New York Living

First published in Great Britain in 1999
by George Weidenfeld & Nicolson

This paperback edition first published in 2000
by Seven Dials, Cassell & Co
Wellington House, 125 Strand
London, WC2R 0BB

A CIP catalogue record for this book is available
from the British Library

ISBN 1 84188 082 5

Designed by: Mark Vernon-Jones
Edited by: Christine Davis
Typeset in: Didot
Printed and bound in Italy

New York Living

LISA LOVATT-SMITH

Photographs by Alberto Heras

SEVEN DIALS

contents

New York, or more accurately its pulsating heart, Manhattan Island, is the oldest continuously inhabited city in America. Covering only 59 square kilometres (22.7 square miles), Manhattan is a vertical city with a somewhat reassuring grid plan at ground level. An inflexible crossword puzzle within an orthogonal mindset, the lines and squares of its geography are a foil to the soaring liberties these islanders take with their skyline and their lifestyles. In the first five minutes after arriving, one despairs of ever understanding New York, overawed as one is by the endless rivers of people sloshing out untidily onto the sidewalk. But after a week or so, the stark and pervasive grid plan becomes oddly comforting, giving the impression that one does in fact know one's way around – it is, after all, as straightforward as knowing how to count. Manhattan is the last great walking city in America, a place where everything is relatively accessible and, for the most part, neatly numbered or labelled. South to north, above Houston Street, are streets 1 to 218; running from east to west are First Avenue to Tenth Avenue. Thus reduced to figures and lines, the city becomes

I carry the place around the world

in my heart but sometimes I try to

shake it off in my dreams.

(F. Scott Fitzgerald)

Introduction

There is something in the New York air that makes sleep useless.

(Simone de Beauvoir)

navigable. Roland Barthes put it beautifully: the grid allows one 'to master the distances and orientations by the mind, to put at one man's disposal the space of these twelve million, this fabulous reservoir, this world emporium in which *all* goods exist except the metaphysical variety.' After a month or so, however, one becomes conscious of the great unwritten laws that govern the grid, and of all the little bits that don't quite fit in. Then one suddenly asks oneself whether one knows New York quite so well after all. F. Scott Fitzgerald compared Fifth and Sixth Avenues to consumer ladders, as did Paul Morand: 'One socially climbs them, like a parrot, with the help of beaks and claws. At thirty, one is at 3oth Street; at seventy, in 7oth Street …' For decades, in the all-important social small print of this most segmented of cities, geographical deviation to either side of the grid has meant discrimination. That has changed now – even the ex-drug-shooting alleys of the neighbourhood known as Alphabet City (because its streets are known as Avenues A, B, C and D) are now residentially desirable. The very speed of change here can be difficult to grasp, as every decade or so the social and ethnic fabric of the different neighbourhoods tends to shift. Until you become a New Yorker – and a New Yorker is something one almost always becomes, rather than being born that way – it is difficult to grasp the subtleties within the abundance of life on the street. It is in the odd-shaped corners where the roads run all higgledy-piggledy, such as Greenwich Village, away from the striped criss-cross regular grid, that artists tend to live and very human things seem to happen – as if the mind is set as free as the street plan. So what makes a New Yorker? Is it when you know that it takes you one minute to walk a block up or down town, and five to walk a block cross town? When you learn to drink cappuccino out of an insulated straw while doing it? When you know that bus transfers will get you anywhere in Manhattan once you bother to study them? Or when you figure out that doubling the tax on a restaurant bill will give you the amount of the tip? Is it the way that New Yorkers still feel the same thrill, even after hundreds of times, when they approach the toy-town skyscrapers of Manhattan

Sometimes, from beyond the skyscrapers, the

cry of a tugboat finds you in your insomnia,

and you remember that this desert of iron

and cement is an island.

(Albert Camus)

New York is the only real city-city.

(Truman Capote)

looming in a surreal manner beyond the vast graveyards on either side of the Queens Expressway? Is it about still being able to perceive the romance in the city that O. Henry called 'Baghdad on the subway' and which, despite its well-documented failings, still has a wealth of redeeming human aspects? Or perhaps a true New Yorker is someone who believes things are somehow more significant when they happen in Manhattan. Be it in art, business, crime, fashion or whatever, if it comes from here it must be the best of its genre. New York has an elusive quality that leads one to believe its myths: that anything can happen, at any time. The city's power of suggestion is equal to none. Is there a contemporary city with greater influence? Probably not. It is not only the modern Babylon but also the modern Athens and Rome. At times its reputation has been so fearfully violent that it has seemed more of a warning than an example, and yet to much of the rest of the world New York *is* America. Everything that this city is, and can be, is firmly imprinted on humankind's collective unconscious – and even if it is the city most seen on

After twenty annual visits, I am still surprised each time I see this giant asparagus bed of alabaster and rose and green skyscrapers.

(Cecil Beaton)

There is no place like it, no place with an atom of its glory, pride, and exultancy. It lays its hand upon a man's bowels; he grows drunk with ecstasy; he grows young and full of glory; he feels that he can never die. (Thomas Wolfe)

celluloid, it rarely disappoints. This book is about 27 New Yorkers' homes, all in Manhattan. Here, more than in any other urban concentration, there is an acute contrast between the free-for-all on the streets and the intimacy of urban interiors. Perhaps, therefore, it would be more exact to say that this book is about the cocoons that people have made for themselves, despite – or perhaps because of – the unceasing, soulless roar caused by the coming and goings of so many. The two worlds of private introspection and public show are drastically opposed. The private universes I have chosen are all extreme in some way – for the most part they are the mirror image, the larger self, the prolongation of the apartment dwellers themselves. Indeed, these disparate NYC interior worlds have that very thing in common: they have been put together by the people themselves, sometimes with the benefit of an architect, but not of a decorator. I have chosen them to be like the city, with all its complicated coded subcultures: extreme. They are here to record just a few of the thousands of different facets of the biggest apple of them all.

The writer and historian Michael Henry Adams lives in one room in deepest Harlem. He calls it the 'late twentieth-century equivalent of an artist's garret' and he is probably right. The early twentieth-century version would have been in Paris, in an area such as Clichy or Montmartre. New York is the current turn-of-the-century's Paris in more ways than one, and Harlem is the only real untapped geographical enigma on the isle of Manhattan. Harlem polarizes New Yorkers: either their smiles freeze or they wax lyrical about the beautiful houses up there; either they begin to warn you against the violence, noise and the impossibility of finding a cab above 110th Street, or they rave about the charms of soul food and the Baptist church services. (Come Sunday, busloads of tourists are accommodated on the churches' first-floor balconies, only to be ushered out after the fun singing bit and before the be-hatted congregation embarks upon its stream-of-consciousness prayers about real issues that might be a bit too much for the visitors to take.) 'Slumming' still seems to exist as a pastime, fifty-odd years after the Cotton Club, Harlem's emblematic 1930s

I

whites-only jazz club, closed. In Manhattan's complex psyche Harlem remains an unresolved issue – as it has been for eighty years, since the start of the African-American colonization of this quiet, seventeenth-century Dutch-built suburb. Just as Brooklyn, that other predominantly black neighbourhood, just beyond the opposite tip of Manhattan, has been colonized by the likes of writers Paul Auster and Tama Janowitz, so New York's intelligentsia, forced out of the traditional residential areas by rising rents and seduced by the lure of more space, has moved into some of the spacious late nineteenth-century and early twentieth-century houses in Harlem's nicer streets. It is a huge area, however, and its architectural riches numerous. Michael Adams' efforts at preservation

are diverse, most of them channelled through his writing and the Upper Manhattan Society for Progress Through Preservation, of which he is chairman. Adams is passionate about his battle against what he terms 'the systematic and partly racist neglect of Harlem over decades and decades'. He has not chosen an easy crusade, as his push to have buildings protected invariably involves complex political and social elements. 'The houses are far finer than even rich people would be able to obtain today,' says Adams. 'You can still find gaslight fixtures in working order, and original coal stoves … It's living history, and a direct consequence of the area having been ostracized in the past.' In order to concentrate on his chosen battle Adams has put aside the usual niceties of life – he does not, for instance, live in one of these handsome buildings himself. Instead he rents a tiny room that he has filled with the few things he considers vital: photographs of his family, a collection of shells, a few well-chosen books, his own drawings of his ideal future home, and little hanging sculptures of cut glass. There is also a closet stuffed to overflowing with his elegant attire, for Adams is a both a dandy and a scholar in the old style, his integrity poignant.

Michael Henry Adams

On the opening pages: a portrait of Michael Henry Adams on the stoop of a traditional house on a Harlem street, and a view of Dutch-style Harlem façades. *On these pages:* The small size of Adam's candlelit apartment adds to the general impression of a riot of precious things. 'I find it hard to limit myself to one particular kind of object or period,' he says. 'Much of my decorating has been about trying to find objects that I like and can afford at the same time. It would be nice for everything to be pristine and perfect, but what has made a lot of these pieces affordable for me is that they are broken and mended. So that, in itself, has become something I like about them. Even if I had billions of dollars I wouldn't change them for anything.'

'I always felt like outcasts belonged in New York,' says Joey Arias, the drag queen star of many infamous Manhattan nights. 'It's always been a big melting pot for artists and all sorts of different people – Andy Warhol, The Factory, freaky superstars – and I'd fantasize about that whole scene. I wanted to be a part of it. My home is in Greenwich Village, overlooking the inside of a block. It's like *Rear Window*, the Alfred Hitchcock film. I sit here and stare out – it's almost as though I'm meditating. It's just how I dreamed Manhattan would be – it's not right in your face. I've always loved that – looking out the windows, looking at other people's lifestyles. I've seen people conceiving children, I've seen the children running around, I see musicians, I see a writer, I see punk kids and dogs, I see everything. Even if I could live in a penthouse I think I would still like this kind of thing, because I like to be surrounded – I don't want to be up looking down. I prefer to live in the dark: I don't like to have light hitting me too much. Darkness is my life, I need to live cave-style. You notice there is no overhead lighting here – I had it all removed. It has to be eye-level or lower. It

2

gives me peace, quiet. I think that when you walk in here it's all about sitting and lying down, it's not about walking around. Some other apartments you want to stand in, kind of pose; you don't really want to sit. Here you do. I wanted to get a kind of Santa Fe atmosphere, because it's also about recharging and relaxing and letting go. I thought these kind of coffee or tobacco walls were symbolic of Santa Fe, while the green on top is mossy, to give it that earthy feeling. I wanted the earth upside-down. The feeling of a boudoir is also something I really like: it's the whore in me, the spider calling the fly to the web, it's my seduction. I love the sensuality of Mae West, Billie Holiday, Betty Page. I like the 1940s, particularly that decade's darker side – the bad girls, all the people who never made it really big. There's a lot of great people. I like portraits, autobiographies of interesting characters, and dolls – I think dolls are like an inner soul, or something that you want to be … There are little bits and pieces of my life here, some of my childhood that I've brought back with me for inspiration. The statue, this African woman, that was from my parents. They were into complete fantasy, forbidden cities – they were pretty wild. Everything was classic 1950s: the zig-zaggy dragon couches and chaise longues with animal skins and incense pots, it was amazing. And then I have art: you know, people have been giving it to me my whole life – Salvador Dali, Andy Warhol, Keith Haring, Kenny Scharf. Years ago I had a few of Jean-Michel Basquiat's drawings and I just threw them in the trash … But now if somebody gives me something I make them sign it, and I have a big collection of art that's tucked away. I've been photographed by Andy Warhol, Thierry Mugler, Keith Haring, Mario Testino, it goes on and on. My mother thought I was going to be a doctor or a football player, and I turned out to be a goddess. I live on Mount Olympus.'

Joey Arias

On the opening pages: a portrait of Joey Arias in front of a Kenny Scharf mixed-media painting, and a detail of another Scharf canvas with a couple of small Warhol pieces. *Above:* a general view of Arias's 'deep bedroom', which he describes as 'an underwater kingdom, inspired by Jules Verne, and an ode to the mermaid lifestyle'. It is dominated by a mixed-media painting, by Stefano Castronovo, of Joey Arias as a sea crea-ture, inspired by Arias's 1986 show 'Mermaids on Heroin'. *Right:* a Mexican cow hide covers a black coffee table that was picked up on the street in nearby Saint Mark's Place. *Opposite:* a view from the sitting room into the bedroom, showing the carefully considered use of colour throughout the space.

Hamish Bowles is a true original, a globe-trot-ting fashion personality whose passion for the decorative and visual arts translates eloquently into his activities as a writer, curator and collector. As well as his very personal assortment of couture frocks – which he has been accumulating more or less since child-hood, and which is now in demand by museums and fashion scholars alike – he has a singular eye for vintage twentieth-cen-tury design. This is apparent in both his Paris and New York apartments. His West Village pied-à-terre is a self-contained base for his frequent trips to the headquarters of American *Vogue*, where he is the highly respected European Editor-at-Large. He chose the 1929 one-bedroomed apartment for both its convenience and, it must be admitted, for its sunken living room, which evokes images of 1930s movie stars descending the three small steps in the best *film noir* mode. Bowles also loved the apartment's sweeping vista over the low-lying Village to the Hudson River. 'It is the first time in my life that I have lived in a building that is not a house. This is a totally new experience for me. I have this bird's-eye view over the

3

boats going by on the river, and to New Jersey beyond. It is an energizing thing. I also loved the fact that it is one of those time-honoured clichéd 1920s apartment buildings.' Characteristically, Bowles refused to furnish the flat as if it were a simple New York stopover, stretching the space to contain an idiosyncratic mix of mid-century Hollywood, 1930s elegance and 1970s chrome. The result is a heady combination of genius and pastiche, with an overall effect that is undeniably glamorous. Bowles can indulge in tat and anecdotal pieces, in gilt and plaster and leopard-skin patterns, because his trained eye brings everything together beautifully. The rooms express not only his appreciation of whimsy but also a sense of humour that stretches to juxtaposing a Syrie Maugham chintz sleigh bed with resolutely contemporary design by friends such as British designer Tom Dixon. Bowles' wide-ranging culture is his best ally: influences as diverse as the dusty decadence of Tangiers in its heyday, the hothouse world of British aesthetes such as Stephen Tennant, David Herbert or Cecil Beaton, or the casual surrealism of Hollywood's best moments, coalesce to create an interior that reflects his most enduring fantasies. This highly individual taste is a quality that Bowles himself most admires in others. His current craze is for the great American decorators of the twentieth century, most of who were brave style innovators themselves, and about whom he is now as knowledgeable as he is about haute couture, his long-standing passion. 'New York is a create-your-own-fantasy sort of a place, where you never know what is going to be behind the next door,' he says. 'There is always that sense of total surprise.' Chez Bowles, the surprise lies in the way great elegance is tempered with an eccentric twist. The apartment's overall effect is both theatrical in the extreme and unabashedly charming – just like its owner.

Hamish Bowles

On the opening pages: a portrait of Hamish Bowles in a 1960s strawberry and cream silk tweed jacket from Bunny Roger's collection. The lamps are late 1930s. The detail shows a Fornasetti table from the late 1960s and a Louis xv chair, upholstered in petunia tweed, in front of a 1970s Karl Springer console table. *On the previous double page:* a general view of the sunken living room. *Opposite:* a detail of the entrance hall with its limed oak mirror by Moreau and a plaster bust light fixture, both from the 1930s. *Below:* a corner of the living room showing a 1940s mirror and an 1860s gilt and gesso Austrian sofa.

Right: a detail of the bathroom 'throne', which is a French *chaise percée.* The towels are from Ralph Lauren. The photographs are Edwardian and were found in a junk shop. *Below:* a corner of the bedroom, showing velum trunks bought at Alfie's Antique Market in London. One hat is from the 1930s; the other was bought in the old quarter of San Juan, Puerto Rico. *Opposite:* a Syrie Maugham sleigh bed and dressing table. The central image is by Rex Whistler and the watercolour on the left is by Cecil Beaton. The chrome bookcases date from the 1970s.

Decorator Muriel Brandolini's Upper East Side brownstone is a trip – a trip to exotic lands, where East and West merge and emerge as something quite different. Inside, the atmosphere is dramatic but playful: each room is saturated with a different colour, and possesses its own mood and identity. Brandolini's background as a fashion stylist has definitely given her the advantage of being perfectly at home with fabric, textures and colours. Her previous apartment, which launched her decorating career, was very much a stage set, with the walls draped in fabric from New York's ethnic neighbourhoods. There she had to use the ruse of a theatrical approach because she was not given leave to paint the walls, but the challenge set her off in the direction that has now become her signature. It calls to mind the rich and voluptuous style of the classic American decorator Rose Cumming, whose interiors always had a delightful touch of the *demi-mondaine* about them while remaining uniformly elegant. Brandolini has become a master at creating intense surroundings, with scant respect for the prevailing purist taste. She is capable of

4

immense grandeur; her mother-in-law, the formidable Christina Brandolini, created her own interiors with the great decorator Renzo Montgardino, and these are without doubt a reference point, yet the essence of Muriel's style is instinctive. In Muriel's home, the oriental ambience of Vietnam – where she lived until the age of twelve – is particularly evident in the deep dark-red dining room on the ground floor. It leads from the much-used kitchen where she and her husband Count Nuno Brandolini – a celebrated *bon viveur* – often officiate.

This is one of the few New York homes where serious epicurean activity is undertaken entirely by the master and mistress of the house. The results are enjoyed by their cosmopolitan crowd of artistic and aristocratic friends. Adjacent is a small patio, which has been transformed into an Eastern-style bamboo grove. Movement around this traditional 1890s house is compulsively vertical, its five floors naturally compartmentalizing different spheres of activity and thus adding to the effect of going from one 'look' to another – the mood changes on every storey. The top floor is the bright and airy domain of the couple's two independently minded and polyglot children, Brando and Filippa. In order to spend as much time as possible with them, their mother has scaled down her business operations so she can work from home. With her inimitable sense of fun she decided to create a colourful universe especially for the children, centred on a fabulous hand-made bunk bed designed to look like a house. On the floor below lies another favourite haunt of the children's: a witty take on the conventional library, this small room is lined with rows and rows of videotapes displayed on shelves just as if they were books. A large day bed sits in front of a screen, which scrolls down from the ceiling – the perfect setting for movie-watching. Beneath it, opposite the *salon* on the first floor, is Brandolini's small boudoir-like office. It is from here that she works according to her very personal principles and business ethic: 'I do what I love. If I don't like the person I don't do it. I have to appreciate the project to be able to take it on. And I love to work from home so that it's easy for me to slip upstairs, lie in bed and play with my children.'

Muriel Brandolini

On the opening pages: a portrait of Muriel Brandolini and her daughter, and a detail of the façades on her Upper East Side street. *On the previous double page:* a view of the mysterious bamboo grove that Brandolini has created in her small garden. *Above:* the dining room features a seventeenth-century bench upholstered in snakeskin-print silk. The lamps above it are Fortuny. *Opposite:* a view of the magnificent red lacquer four-poster bed which has been placed in the dining room, so one can recline after supper. The portrait is of Brandolini's husband, Count Nuno, as a child. *Left:* a detail of the kitchen, where more informal suppers are served.

On these pages: the sitting room. *Opposite:* a contemporary painting by Donald Baechler hangs over the fireplace. The card table and slip chair in *petit point* are both nineteenth-century. *Above:* painted a subtle *vert de nil*, the room has the atmosphere of a winter garden. The Allegra Hicks carpet has been chosen in the same spirit. The detail, left, shows a George Condo painting above a nineteenth-century sofa upholstered in mauve.

Right: a detail of the entrance, showing the stairway that runs like a backbone through the house. The Chinese lamp was bought in Hong Kong. The drawing is by George Condo and the chair is 1920s. *Below:* a view of the bathroom, draped with fine embroidered linen; the walls are covered with fabric by Brandolini. Beyond is a walk-in dressing room. *Opposite:* Muriel Brandolini's cosy office, where she keeps her many art books and part of her collection of contemporary photographs. The crystal and silk hanging is Venetian, by Pier Lorenzo.

Opposite: a corner of the master bedroom, in deep coral, which is dominated by a chinoiserie armoire and a contemporary mixed-media painting by Donald Baechler. *Left:* the bed, which is made up with pretty embroidered linen, is flanked by two lamps found in a flea market. Above hang two prints by Constantin Kakanias. *Above left:* a view of the landing, looking through to the master bedroom. The antique cupboard reflects Brandolini's appreciation of the oriental aesthetic. *Above:* the Brandolinis' two children in their extraordinary bunk bed-cum-play house designed by Muriel Brandolini. The paper lamp is by Tom Dixon.

The East Village, on the fringes of Alphabet City, is fast becoming genteel – even though it would have been unthinkable as a desirable residential area a decade ago. Except, of course, to the notoriously unconventional Greek-born photographer Calliope, who moved there at around that time. She adored the variety, exoticism and rawness of an area that has always readily accepted immigrants and artists; she is both, and she does not scare easily. Her building, which dates from 1800, was converted from a rough hotel-cum-shelter in the style of the infamous Bowery flop houses. 'This area and this building are very bohemian and carefree,' she says. 'It's very me, because I'm not at all an uptown type of person.' To look at Calliope is to catch a glimpse of a certain a kind of eternal feminine breed: beyond her jangling bracelets and other hippie accoutrements she has a stirring beauty straight out of Delacroix, the easy sensuality of an orientalist's muse. Adding to this effect is the fact that she dresses as if her role in a previous lifetime might have been as the ivory-skinned prize odalisque in a very grand sultan's seraglio. She has adopted the

5

deep, vibrant colours of the East, and her silk kaftans are made up in India to her own designs. Her deliciously serene appearance is deceptive: as one of the world's foremost photographers of children, and the instigator of a very personal style in that particular branch of photography, Calliope has the non-stop life of an international businesswoman. When visiting her wonderfully decadent apartment, however, it is easy to think that she does nothing but sip sherbet and nibble Turkish delight while dispensing her famous hospitality. The floods of visitors are easily seduced by their first encounter with the low-slung L-shaped living room-cum-office. The

atmosphere is overwhelmingly feminine, and the mood restful to the extreme. On opening the door, the first thing one meets is a domestic-style altar, comprising dozens of fresh flowers and candles, stuck in old vases and candle holders, in front of an ancient pock-marked mirror. 'It was important to me to create a corner where I could group together everything that is sacred. I believe that God is everywhere so I have all kinds of divinities, and make them little offerings.' It is a reminder that one is entering a space where stress and self-imposed conventions have to be left at the door – from now on the visitor is in Calliope's aura. 'I moved to New York in 1986 and I adore it. There is no place like this that gives people from all over the world the freedom to express themselves. Although I still love Europe, I feel more at ease here. This house reflects my personality: the bits and pieces have mostly been brought back from my travels, and the house kind of formed itself instinctively around me.' Just how much Calliope has to travel is reflected in her finds from as far afield as Pakistan, Morocco, Turkey and her native Greece as well as India, which has been a major influence and is her favourite shopping destination of them all.

Calliope

On the opening pages: a portrait of Calliope, reclining on an eighteenth-century Provençal bed with fake fur bolsters from Morocco. The detail shows part of the terrace she created. *Left:* Calliope's home 'altar', which is covered with antique Moroccan hand-embroidery; many different deities are represented. The mirror is sixteenth-century and was bought at an auction at Christie's. *Below:* eighteenth-century Venetian mirrored candleholders are hung on the wall, which Calliope has stencilled with Islamic motifs. The cushions are mostly Ottoman, from the eighteenth and nineteenth century. *Opposite:* an eighteenth-century Central Asian tapestry hanging dominates the living room.

Gerard Dalmon has a very anecdotal, very New York yarn about his Chelsea apartment. With a twinkle in his eye, he waves expansively at the sunny space around him and lowers his voice theatrically: 'This used to be a *back room.*' What was once a VIP encounters room for the reckless patrons of the infamous and happening 1980s nightclub Area, is now an intensely personal space. The biggest ingredient in Dalmon's decorating scheme is a sense of fun: he is not afraid of either deep kitsch or outspoken colour. The result is explosive: silver hydrogen balloons cover the bedroom ceiling, collections of toys jostle for space on the shelves, and the different walls of the rooms are painted odd and not necessarily complementary colours. But Dalmon is able to carry off his wacky interior with aplomb, since the whole scheme is grounded with good pieces of contemporary design by the European designers whom he favours. Dalmon was in fact one of the two pioneering partners of the French furniture gallery Neotu, which was founded in 1985 and has since gone from strength to strength, serving as a rallying point for design in an otherwise

6

hardly vigorous Parisian context. Neotu has a highly independent approach: the name itself is a word play, meaning 'neo-everything', and is a tongue-in-cheek reference to the widespread obsession with categorizing artists' work according to prevailing movements such as primitivism, minimalism, rationalism and so on. Neotu's aim was never to embrace only one style, and the gallery's refreshingly heterogeneous approach led to an outlet in New York, where Dalmon has been living since 1994. His apartment, naturally enough, thus doubles as an incidental showroom for some of the most interesting work by contemporary designers and decorative artists. The large tree-like lamps (by design duo Garouste and Bonetti) that define the main living space, for example, are temporary refugees from rock star Lou Reed's mostly Neotu-designed interior, and the odd cardboard box contains pieces en route to and from exhibitions. The knowledge that his modest space would soon be filled with the spectacular creations favoured by

the gallery did not prompt Dalmon to choose a neutral colour scheme. When he moved in, the whole place was white. The very first thing he did was custom-mix a yellowy green tone for certain walls, a bright yellow for others and a pale blue for another, plus a vibrant orange for the trim. Then he installed shelves in the narrow passageway, to display his vast collection of toys from the 1940s and 50s. Finally, before moving in Neotu's wonderful creations, Dalmon and his partner Joseph Savastano threw an enormous party for Valentine's Day; the extravagant preparations included filling the still-empty apartment with 200 plastic roses and plastic-flower cushions. This was the beginning of a party tradition whereby four times a year – for Bastille Day, Hallowe'en and Christmas as well as Valentine's Day – the space is transformed into another kind of imaginary paradise, very much in line with Dalmon's ebullient approach to life.

Gerard Dalmon

On the opening pages: a portrait of Gerard Dalmon, and a detail of the entrance to his apartment. Lined with shelves displaying some of his extensive toy collection, it prepares the visitor for Dalmon's 'pop' approach. *On these pages:* the living room. *Left:* The tree-branch lamp, one of a pair by Garouste and Bonetti, was originally made for Lou Reed. The dining table and chairs are also by Garouste and Bonetti, as is the tufted red velvet sofa, above. The art work is by Felix Gonzales Torres, and the yellow lamp is by Pucci de Rossi.

Above: detail of a desk designed by Gerard Dalmon. Hanging above it is a photograph of a moose by Larry Gianettino. The brightly coloured fountain is by Pucci de Rossi and the pebble lamps are from the 1960s. *Left:* a tree-branch side table by Aaron Kllc stands next to a chair by Garouste and Bonetti. The black and white painting is by Annette Lemieux and the photograph next to it is by Catherine Nance. *Opposite:* the living room is anchored by a textured, brightly coloured wool and metal carpet, of recent design, and a red leather armchair by Olivier Gagnère, produced in a limited edition for Neotu. The cabinet is by Eric Schmitt, the green sofa is by Martin Szekely and the bronze coffee table is by Garouste and Bonetti.

Opposite: with a nod to 1960s aesthetics, amoeba-shaped mirrors have been stuck to the doors of the full-length closets in the bedroom. *Above:* the bedspread and dangling silk-tassel lamp were designed by Dalmon using the same amoeba-like motif. The bedside lamps are by Sylvie Cogranne, right, and Franc Palaia, left. The Daliesque 'melting clock' is by Nicolas Cortes and Jim Seffens. *Right:* part of Dalmon's extensive toy and snow-scene collection, displayed in the bathroom.

When asked how he turned the shell of his SoHo warehouse conversion into a home, Giorgio Deluca loves to kid: 'I just threw in my bed and all the equipment I had, and that was it.' He actually moved in before the steel that was to frame the windows had been delivered, in December 1995, so for the first couple of months he had to tiptoe through little piles of snow when he woke up in the morning to get from his bed to the bathroom. Fortunately life has become a little less spartan since then, in fact it has evolved into quite a sybaritic existence. While it is certainly true that the impact of the space is mostly architectural, and that it relies on large expanses of empty floor for its effect, there is more to this bright, white loft space than first meets the eye. Firstly, there is the wonderfully equipped kitchen. This serves as a laboratory for Deluca who, with his partner Joe Dean and Jack Ceglic, founded Dean & Deluca, the world-famous food emporium which has revolutionized the way trendy New Yorkers eat in (on the rare occasions they do). Deluca has a fine collection of cookery books and appliances, and a generous dining table, while bowls

7

overflowing with corks testify to the good use made of the floor-to-ceiling wine rack. Secondly, there is the cleverly designed garden, on the penthouse roof, which commands a sweeping view of the green Jersey shore and the Hudson River. The garden comes complete with sun decks, rambling roses, outdoor shower and pocket-handkerchief lawn. Then there is the bed, placed in front of French doors that give onto the terrace. These attractive arrangements are the result of a great deal of work, for this was previously an abandoned building. It may once have been a sausage-casing factory and was certainly a warehouse from 1908 onwards, when the wooden infrastructure was replaced by a steel and concrete frame. This was lucky for Deluca, whose landscaped garden and heavy terracotta plant pots could never have been installed on top of a

building which only had wooden beams. Deluca bought the whole building, kept the top floor and sold off the rest to other would-be loft-dwellers. Together with architect John Fifield he decided to leave the downstairs level relatively bare, with cabinetry along the kitchen wall, a concrete cooking island and a flying concrete staircase. Upstairs, the scale is much more intimate: the bathroom, bedroom, dressing room, shower room and hallway have more conventional proportions and give a feeling of intimacy to the private quarters. The garden, with its four separate areas, echoes this arrangement, its secluded corners perfect for Deluca's celebrated Italian-style alfresco entertaining.

Giorgio G. Deluca

On the opening pages: a portrait of Giorgio Deluca and a detail of his impressive rooftop garden with its views of TriBeCa and the river beyond. *On the previous double page:* a view of the main space in the duplex showing the floating staircase, the long kitchen island and a 1940s-style bentwood chair made out of a single piece of plywood. Deluca created the coffee table himself, from a wine rack and a piece of glass. The sofas were made to measure, and the 1950s bar stools were designed by Harry Bertoia for Knoll. *Left:* a corner of the same space, showing the cast-iron stove. *This page:* two details of the kitchen, which is crammed with professional cooking tools and appliances of every description.

Left: Deluca's outdoor shower falls onto well-drained teak floorboards in a secluded corner of the terrace. *Below:* a view of Deluca's bed, seen from the garden. He wakes up every day to an imposing view over the Hudson. The bedside tables, which hold CDS, were designed by Deluca. The two deep cherry Charles and Ray Eames' LCW plywood chairs to the left are a 1946 design. *Below left:* a view of the bathroom with its modern German claw-foot bath. *Opposite:* the teak and iron garden furniture is designed to resist the extreme New York weather. The garden is planted with an exuberant mixture of Mediterranean plants including lavender, sage and summer clematis.

From the bustle of the garment district in Midtown – with its incessant traffic, frantic wholesalers and shops spilling over onto the street – to the controlled calm of Han Feng's loft is only a short elevator ride, but the journey provides one of the strange contrasts that are so common in New York. High above the chasm of the roaring street, a Zen-like space of blinding whiteness has been cleverly incorporated into an industrial shell. Translucent white gauze hangs from all the windows and also separates the different 'rooms' from each other, transforming the whole living area into a glowing cube of soft, filtered light. The space is pure without being minimalist by virtue of the organic elements that can be found in corners or lined up across the stone floor: giant dried pods, a ball made of twisted branches, five huge pebbles, orchids everywhere. The shiny black of a grand piano and plenty of dark, oriental-looking antiques (which are actually Viennese Secessionist) give an element of drama and contrast. A large pot, with a cracked eggshell celadon glaze, is home to a busy handful of bright red fish. There is a deafening sound of bird song,

8

as the culprits hop from perch to perch in a collection of antique bamboo cages hung high on the walls far away from the feline force of José the cat, with his triangular features, oversized ears and insidious casual affection. Another cat, and a friendly photogenic Labrador called Cheyenne, also share the space with Chinese-born fashion designer Han Feng. She arrived in New York from Shanghai in 1985. After a stint as a shop girl at Bloomingdales, almost by accident she began designing scarves which were snapped up by the exclusive store Henri Bendel. With the store's encouragement she progressed to designing outfits and before long had become a fully-fledged designer, showing her first collection in 1993. Like her home – which has very few actual Far Eastern pieces, but feels very oriental – her clothes are 'East–West mixed'. She says of her apartment: 'You don't really see the East, you only feel it. People always come in here and say "I love your Asian furniture", yet most of it is

Viennese.' Her home relies heavily on the dramatic use of fabric. 'The space has become very concentrated, very focused, because of the use of fabrics and drapes. The clothes I design are also about draping, shrouding – the cut and the movement make the effect.' When Feng found her loft it was a five-roomed warehouse conversion with wallpaper, wall-to-wall carpeting and windows blocked by bookcases. She set about her transformation by going back to basics and establishing what, for her, was important: a large, light-drenched bathroom; a private bedroom (the only room that is screened off with more than fabric) and a kitchen from where she could entertain easily. She is a multicultural gourmet: 'I don't cook specifically Chinese things – I was brought up during the Cultural Revolution, where we were taught to embrace uniformity and modernity. So sometimes when I'm asked to cook, like for Chinese New Year, I actually have to go to the library and learn about all my supposed traditions the hard way!'

Han Feng

On the opening pages: a portrait of Han Feng in her New York loft; the detail shows a pair of antique Chinese doors and a Josef Hoffmann rocking chair. *Below:* the small card table and chairs are all Wiener Werkstätte, the Vienna-based movement which formed around Hoffmann in the early years of the twentieth century. The cotton drapes were bought in Chinatown; they were originally designed as mosquito nets. *Left:* A Burmese cat, one of Han Feng's numerous pets, on the grand piano. *Opposite:* the embossed leather chairs, dining table and black lacquered chairs are also Wiener Werkstätte. Han Feng is particularly attracted to this style of design, perhaps because of its strong oriental influence.

Left: a view of the bedroom, where José the cat has evidently made himself comfortable. Han Feng's collection of antique birdcages and black and white photographs is spread around the apartment. The flamboyant yellow bedside lamp is from the New York store Shanghai Tang. The small bamboo foot-stool was bought in Chinatown. *Above:* the bust was a flea market find and the theatrical-looking pearl necklace is a piece from one of Han Feng's early collections.

Above: a view of the romantic bathroom with its vintage bath-tub. The candles and orchids add to the contemplative atmosphere. The red silk ball was designed by Han Feng. *Opposite:* as befits Han Feng's concept of free flowing space, the bathroom is separated from this sitting room area by nothing more than a thin cotton curtain. The side table is by Josef Hoffmann, and the dressmaker's dummy seen in the background is wearing a wedding dress designed by Han Feng.

A fascinating discovery lies at the heart of style journalist Amy Fine Collins's rambling Park Avenue apartment: a plethora of concealed clothes closets. They are a homage to two very different men – neither of whom, it must be said, is her husband. (He has 'altogether more serious pursuits'.) Collins is muse to and passionate collector of Geoffrey Beene, that master of liquid geometry and godfather of American modernism in fashion. She has the perfect figure for the role. Tall, lithe and languid, like a cameo from the Jazz Age, she wears his bias-cut iconoclastic creations with verve. Beene does not design for the norm, and in Collins he has found an exceptional advocate who does not require the usual conventions of late twentieth-century dress codes to validate her style. Sartorially experimental, she displays to perfection Mr Beene's maverick approach. The other man in her closet is one with whom she is on first-name terms: his creations are only ever referred to as 'Manolos'. These, of course, are the beaded, feathered, delicate and altogether charming concoctions by Manolo Blahnik, the international Sultan of the Shoe. Her eyes twinkling,

9

Collins confesses to only very rarely having the odd illegitimate fashion affair and slipping her feet into something different or wearing clothes designed by others. That, however, remains an occasional indulgence – generally it is Mr Beene and Manolo or nothing, as reflected ad infinitum by the mirrors on the closet doors. Her involvement with the arts, which ultimately led her to fashion, began 'as soon as I could think and see. My mother was an artist, and became an art historian. She was always very aware of anything aesthetic and visual, and as a child I was dragged around museums, antique stores and auctions.' After teaching Art History, Fine Collins decided to concentrate on art criticism for glossy American magazines. For the last ten years she has been mainly seduced by the decorative arts, having become one of the prestigious special correspondents at *Vanity Fair*. It was through her first piece of fashion journalism that she met Mr Beene, while writing of his twenty-five year retrospective. She approached the exhibition as if it were high art. 'I reviewed the show as if I were writing about an art show because that was what I had been trained to do, and I guess the approach must have struck him. We have been friends ever since.' Her handsome, classically proportioned apartment – restored by architect Robert Couturier – has equally taken its tone from the subjects that Collins writes about. Like most of her themes of choice, 'everything is from the time block that goes from the First World War to

1970 – there is nothing really contemporary. Helena Rubinstein's influence is all over the place. I wrote about her houses, did a lot of research on her and admire her taste enormously. Many things are similar to those she had in her apartment.' Refreshingly, whimsical colours abound in her roomsets as well as in her closet. 'I think colour is the emotional part of design. There are no intrinsically ugly colours; everything rests in knowing how to combine them.'

Amy Fine Collins

On the opening pages: a portrait of Amy Fine Collins, with her daughter. She is wearing a dress by Geoffrey Beene; her make-up is by Carlo Garaci and her hair by Yves Durif. The detail shows violet plumes displayed in the living room. *On the previous double page:* the living room in its entirety. The carpet in the foreground is 1970s Pucci, handmade in Argentina; the silver-gilt chair is 1920s Venetian. *Left:* a view of the dining room where three contemporary chairs by Mario Villa line up against a wall hung with part of Amy Fine Collins's collection of fashion images. The chairs have been upholstered with Gene Meyer silk scarves. *Below:* a 1930s plaster mirror and console bought in a Paris flea market.

Above: a view of the bedroom. Like the dining room chairs, the banquette at the foot of the bed has also been upholstered with Gene Meyer scarves. The bedroom contains many references to the fashion designer Elsa Schiaparelli. The watercolour on the bedside table is by Marcel Vertès for a Schiaparelli advertisement; the screen behind the chaise longue is by also by Vertès, from around 1950. On the bed there is even a box of vintage Schiaparelli stockings which were recently found in a provincial store. *Opposite:* a partial view of Amy Fine Collins's closets showing part of her extensive collection of Manolo Blahnik shoes.

The ebullient editor, resident guardian angel and creator of the New York cutting-edge magazine *Paper* has assembled a highly personal space of her own, perched high above Washington Square. After walking through the just-so lobby of a well-manicured mid-century block, the apartment comes as something of a shock. It is as funky as its occupant, who has evidently allowed herself to indulge her sense of humour during the decorating process. Crammed with modern art and pieces of rigorously contemporary design, the place is pure pop – from the door mat that says 'go away', to the fridge that is covered with a impressive selection of kitsch magnets. Witty, challenging and provocative, it is like a wide-open window onto Hastreiter's soul, a reflection of her most intimate tastes and fantasies. This small but spacious one-bedroom pad pays homage to a certain American sensibility of the 1950s and 60s, an era when shag-pile carpet was all the rage and furnishings began to explore new shapes and textures. At this time, to be modern was to be bold, and the domestic home was the site for the explosion of a completely new visual language.

In terms of innovation, the period has hardly been bettered since. This boxy apartment, painted a warm white as a foil to the colours, patterns and general accumulation of art and artefacts it contains, dates from the same era. Hastreiter's choices have been very deliberate: visual editing is as much a part of her life as words are, and her home benefits from her informed selection of what is now seen as timeless great design. Her main motivation, however, is emotional. The apartment is packed with her mother's furniture and she even called up the architect who had designed the interiors of her childhood and commissioned him to recreate them several decades later. 'I grew up with these huge, long L-shaped couches, which he built in for us, where all the family would sprawl, and as soon as I saw this space I said, "I need one of those …". I also covered it in bright plaids the way my mother used to.' Hastreiter started out on her New York odyssey in 1976 when she moved into a tenement apartment in SoHo, later graduating to one of the first real lofts in TriBeCa. Twenty years later, by which time lofts had become mainstream and TriBeCa desirable, she was ready to move on and find herself a 'grown-up space' – a real apartment with separate rooms and even uniformed doormen. She was picky; being both determined to live in Greenwich Village but also accustomed to the glorious spaces of her loft, the process understandably took forever. It was the views of the Twin Towers, together with the pocket-handkerchief terrace (which she has turned into a vegetable-bearing mini-jungle) which finally persuaded her to choose this apartment, despite the fact that it was then shabby and cramped, and that its interior layout needed to be completely reworked. This, then, is her mature space, despite (or perhaps because of) the delightful madness in her choices. Indeed, her taste has remained as wild and wacky as the lifeblood of gossip, hot news and vibrant style journalism that she pumps into *Paper* magazine every month.

Kim Hastreiter

On the opening pages: a portrait of Kim Hastreiter, and the view from her rooftop terrace. *Opposite:* a Noguchi dining table and Arne Jacobsen chairs. The bar stools are by Harry Bertoia for Knoll. *Below:* a view through the dining-room hatch into the kitchen, which is crammed with quirky objects. *On the following double page:* vintage 1960s fabric covers the built-in sofa designed by Milton Klein. The surfboard table is by Charles Eames and was bought at a flea market. The blue chair on the left is a Harry Bertoia Bird chair; the red chair with footstool is a Knoll Womb chair, designed by Eero Saarinen. The art work on the left, *Hello My Name is Satan*, is by Erik Brunetti.

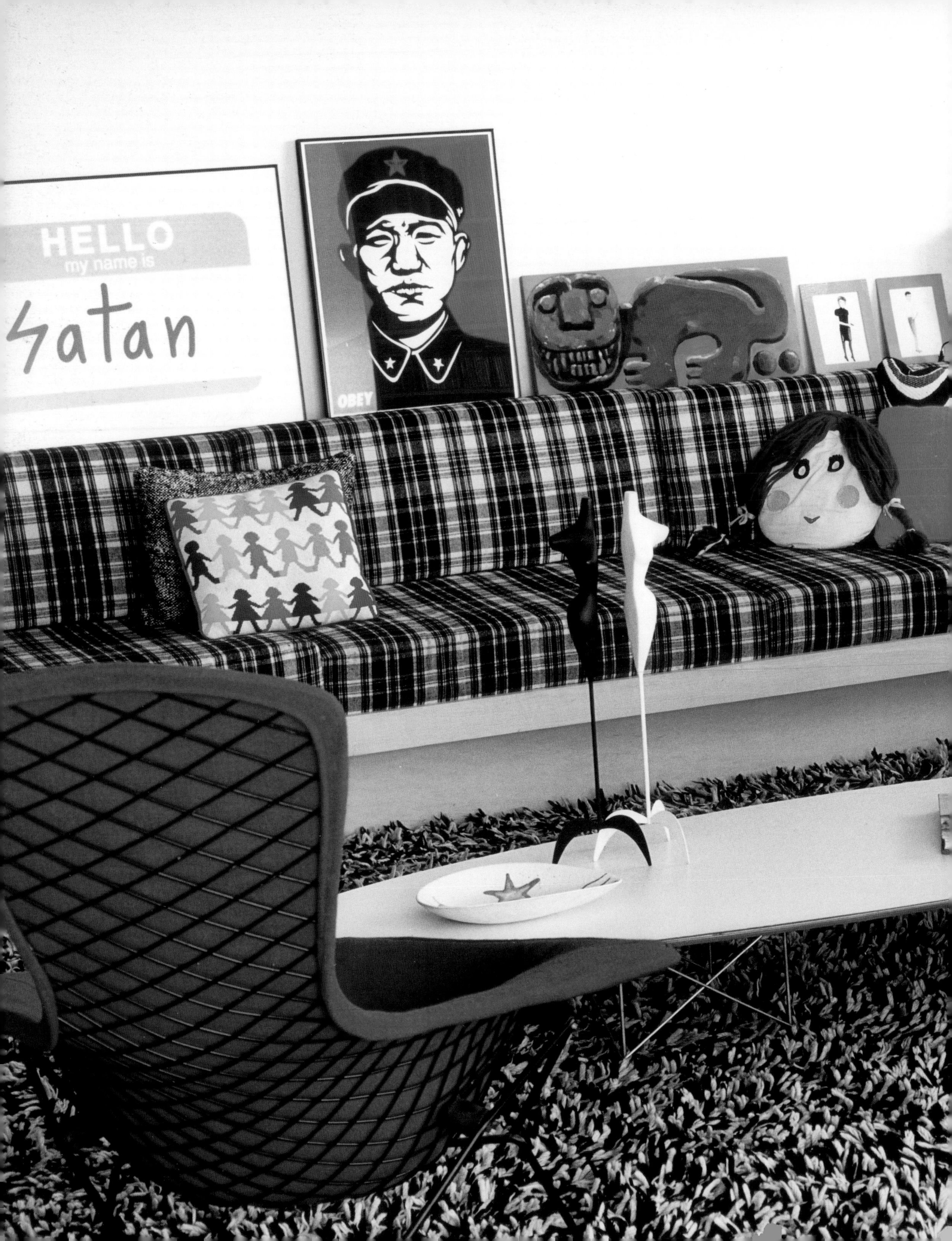
HELLO
my name is
Satan
OBEY

Above: a partial view of the bedroom, showing the Dunbar day bed that was one of Hastreiter's favourite refuges as a child and was a present from her mother. The photograph is by Seydou Keïta. The twig bed, made in Colorado, came from a West Coast swap meet. Chris Lehrecke made the dresser as well as the bookshelves, shown above right. The portraits of US presidents were found in the flea market on 26th Street. *Right:* a view of the bathroom, with its black and white tiles. *Opposite:* another view of the bedroom, showing a Charles Eames chair in the foreground. The paintings to the left are by Phil Frost, and the large photograph is by Nick Waplington.

This is Joseph Holtzman's nest. It has more than a passing similarity to *Nest*, the upbeat, luxuriously alternative shelter magazine that Holtzman produces – mostly from his sofa. This beautifully presented and wacky periodical, which has worldwide cult status, is busy, batty and boisterous – just like Holtzman's Upper East Side interior. *Nest* has featured such unmissable pieces as prison interiors, igloos, and the Brooklyn pad of a Farrah Fawcett-fixated fan who had papered his entire interior with pictures of the *Charlie's Angels* star. The magazine is a provocative, humorous take on the self-obsessed world of interior decorating, as perceived through the acerbic prism of Holtzman's ready intelligence. Yet this soft-spoken Baltimore boy loves decoration with a compulsive passion, and although *Nest* sends it up, it also celebrates it. Holtzman's own apartment definitely qualifies for inclusion: it is a fine example of personality grafted onto walls and rooms. Here he has clearly elevated decor to the stature of installation art. In the words of his partner Carl Skoggard, who recently wrote a tongue-in-cheek piece for *Nest* entitled 'Yes, I too married

II

a decorator…': 'Our insouciant mingle is not unlike the refined eclectic clutter of a knowledgeable late Victorian home.' Skoggard compares living with Holtzman to sharing space with a creative volcano, and comments: 'You may go on wishing that your visible surroundings were fixed and permanent, but in your heart you know they aren't.' The apartment shifted from pop minimal to its present incarnation without warning. 'I was particularly disturbed the day my twenty-four-hour domestic demiurge began covering all the white surfaces of our apartment with layer upon layer of prints and paintings, rugs and textiles,' recalls Skoggard. 'Then he started overpainting wallpaper and ceilings with variable black grids, and "photo tiling" other walls with a repeating laminated photograph. But now I've started to think that white walls look bleached and naked. They just stand there embarrassed, not knowing what to do. I do like our busy full-time walls.' Holtzman's home is a total environment, which he has layered in a compulsive manner with things that are meaningful to him. 'However incongruous they might be, the objects I love belong together,' he says. 'Occasionally the way they share space can become metaphorically suggestive, even comical – which is something I enjoy very much indeed.' The result is a bewilderingly intense patchwork of colour and form, with every surface gloriously cluttered with pedigree *tchotchkes*, great art or painstaking collage. It is a self-contained universe, far removed from the genteel neighbourhood outside the window. (Holtzman hates to go out: he is compulsively interior-minded and slightly agoraphobic.) In his characteristic self-deprecating way Holtzman advertises the fact that his tiny staff like to call him the 'python' because he spends most of his time in bed or in the bath. Skoggard is kinder: Holtzman is 'a restless talent on easy terms with connoisseurship, who delights in the tactful subversion of convention, innocent visual violence, odd placement and delayed discovery.' Holtzman, decorator and editor, often asks himself the rhetorical question: if he were to be confined to one room forever, how would he make it bearable? Both *Nest* and this nest are his answer.

Joseph Holtzman

On the opening pages: a portrait of Joseph Holtzman sitting on the sofa where he says he spends most of his time. The detail shows one of Holtzman's many *objects de curiosité. Opposite:* a view of the living room. The painting above the sofa is by Dubuffet and the coffee table is by Alchimia; the blue leather chair, one of a pair, is George II. *Below:* a Matisse statue stands in the centre of the room, in front of a magnificent 1957 Rothko canvas. The improbable juxtaposition of high and low art in Holzman's confined space gives the apartment much of its impact. The blue stripes on the walls were applied with a mixture of beeswax and pigment.

On these pages: 'I don't like one-liner rooms that reveal themselves too quickly. I like subtle discovery and depth …' The dining room reflects Holtzman's creed perfectly, as seen in the wall and ceiling detail, above, and general view, opposite. The combination of colours, geometrical shapes and objects gives the room a complexity that is most unexpected in such a small space. Strong patterns counteract the room's architectural limitations, making it appear to be one huge visual labyrinth.

Opposite: the bathroom is the work of artist Patrick O'Brien, as are many of the other paint effects in the apartment. Joseph Holtzman enjoys promoting new talent and although O'Brien is a 'serious' artist he rose to the challenge of this unusual decorative proposal. In the bathroom he was given carte blanche, and the result is a particularly unusual combination of spots, stripes and wiggles. The stone poodle supporting the basin is a witty reference to Holtzman's dog. *Above:* a detail of the bedroom, which Holtzman also uses as an office. The paint effects and patterns are as intense here as they are elsewhere in the apartment, and provide an interesting contrast to the neoclassical painting of a male nude.

Artist Judith Hudson is a refugee from loft living. 'At one point, in the city I lived in a place that was made for machines, and in the country I lived in a place that was made for animals. I desperately wanted to live in a place that was made for humans for a change – you know, with doorways and mouldings and places to hide. Especially since a loft is rather like a bathtub – you all end up by the drain, so to speak. Despite having masses of space, the whole family was always in one place huddled together on the bed, or the sofa, writing, working, watching TV … Eventually it got to the point where the kids wanted their privacy and I wanted mine.' The generous 1850 Gramercy Park house they subsequently moved into, which is documented as having once been a brothel, among other things, possesses a sense of space that is rare in New York. 'It had the right scale, like a painting. I felt I could work with it.' It has rooms, and nooks and crannies and broom-cupboards and stairs. And more stairs. It is the perfect antidote to a loft. 'The loft was all views and light, whereas this is all about interiors, introspection.' What is more, it is a proper functioning family

12

home, considerably enlivened by the presence of Hudson's two tearaway teenage daughters who, with their inseparable paraphernalia such as skateboards, roller blades, funky music and a tribe of friends, make the place come alive. Thus the first-floor lounge, despite its serious art and its fragile embroidered fabrics, is no stiff reception room but rather a vital chill-out zone, and the imposing stainless-steel kitchen really is used to cook up quantities of chow while the kids do their homework perched at the counter. Decorating is obviously one of Hudson's many talents – although the family have lived here for only three years, the house seems irrevocably shaped and moulded to reflect her own very personal style. It's a great place to spend time, partly because every room has been approached in a very individual way, so that behind the shiny red paint of the front door there are a myriad different worlds. On the ground floor is the post-industrial kitchen, adjacent to a fair-sized yard which has a distinctly exotic flavour, perhaps because of the deep blue embroidered sun umbrella from India which matches the walls. It feels more like Bogota, Havana or Seville than the Lower East Side. On the first floor, the library-cum-dining room has 1930s furniture and walls lined with books; on the next floor the master bedroom is definitely colonial in feel, while the bathroom is pure original Art Deco. On the kids' floor, at the very top of the house, the vibe is definitely Moroccan. It could seem like a terminal case of mixed metaphors but Hudson's trained, painterly eye has ensured that the palette and a certain modernity of touch are consistent throughout. What could have been a muddle is a triumph, as it has all been done with a very light hand and plenty of Hudson's ready humour and talent for irreverent interpretation.

Judith Hudson

On the opening pages: a portrait of Judith Hudson's youngest daughter. The detail shows a Chinese chest of drawers in the entrance hall, a painting by Alfred Jensen, and a Tibetan rug. *Opposite:* a detail of the yard, with its wrought-iron gallery outside the first-floor dining room. The embroidered umbrella comes from India. *Below:* the kitchen, recently installed by Hudson, features ultramodern industrial brushed stainless-steel and zinc surfaces.

Opposite: a view from the living room through to the stairwell. The original decorative paint effects on the walls, discovered during the building's restoration, have been left visible. The chaise longue has been upholstered in yellow velvet curtain material. *Above:* the library-cum-dining room. The chairs are 1930s, the table is American country. The fireplace is original to the house but its neo-classical detailing is probably of later date. *Left:* a corner of the living room. *On the following double page:* a general view of the same room, showing a canvas by Julian Schnabel, left, and three paintings by Judith Hudson. The unusual double-sided sofa successfully centres the room.

Left: the bed in the main bedroom originally belonged to Hudson's mother; by extraordinary coincidence she found it for sale some years after her death. The bedspread is from the Philippines, and the painting is by Judith Hudson. *Above:* the eldest daughter of the house in the bathroom, which features spectacular underwater murals and unusual twin baths. Hudson discovered that the bathroom had been designed in the 1930s by the then owners of the house so that the husband – who was a prominent diplomat – could discuss with his wife the ideas that came to him while bathing. The revelation of this fact apparently caused something of a scandal amongst the conservative public at the time.

Above: a detail of the girls' bathroom with a pair of Indian mirrors over a vintage double sink. The light fixtures are nineteenth-century. *Opposite:* the Moroccan striped room, which is the bedroom of one of the girls. Artist Ricky Clifton painstakingly created the pattern and texture using a collage of coloured paper. The room rather beautifully evokes the atmosphere of a Moroccan tent.

There is definitely a Cinderella aspect to the story of this abandoned chorizo factory-turned-town house in the West Village. There is a touch of the magic wand in the way the transformation came about, and something of the chic fairy godmother in actress Karen Lashinsky's dramatic looks. Most tellingly of all, however, the building is like a stage-set ready and waiting, with the huge, rambling kitchen – more Tuscan than Gotham – being the 'before the ball' scene, and the silk- and satin-strewn boudoir and massive chateau-style chimney breast being most certainly 'after'. Although Lashinsky could envisage the potential of this dark, rotting factory, with no electricity or water supply, and dangerously damaged floors, its transformation into a home required more than simple restoration and decoration. On acquiring the building Lashinsky conjured up an inspired *coup de théâtre*: she took the bold decision to order the centre of the house to be removed, thus losing a quarter of the building's floor space but gaining a lofty 10-metre (32-foot) atrium in order to let light and air into the tall, narrow structure. This has added immensely to the house's charm.

13

The courtyard is disconcerting because of the sheer theatrical impact of its unexpected soaring height, and the sense of space it conveys. An architectural feature that is most uncommon in New York, the courtyard 'centres' the structure – as in Islamic or Spanish Colonial architecture – and all other living spaces lead out of it. 'At the same time as I was restoring the house I was performing with The Wooster Group [an experimental theatre company] all over the world, in Hong Kong, Holland, Colombia … When you are working like that, you get to go into some very funky buildings. I took a lot of photographs; I used to love fantasizing about what I saw and how I would incorporate it into this house, buying things at flea markets as I went along. The courtyard was inspired by the Mediterranean and South America – I love the idea of houses with their inside removed to make an outside … If it hadn't been snowy old New York, I would have taken the roof off.' Lashinsky is something of a visionary where interior design is concerned. She likes salvage, recuperation, adaptation; she loves patinas, rust, age – all of which required much explanation to the workers on the house. ('With the workmen, it got to the point where they would pick stuff out of the garbage, brandish it at me inquiringly, say "Antique?" and laugh …') The monumental staircase, for example, which snakes its way around the atrium, was built to fit the banister which she had salvaged from a hotel, and the two arched doorways to her and her daughter Juliet's bedroom suites were built around two extravagant doors they had found on the pavement years ago in Canal Street. The kitchen sink was discovered in the basement, the venerable floorboards were simply restored and laid down again, and the factory cabinets were recast as part of the kitchen. The result of this unconventional attitude is a hauntingly beautiful home quite unlike any other, a stage-set for living inspired and adapted by Lashinsky's own unique decorating concepts.

Karen Lashinsky

On the opening pages: a portrait of Karen Lashinsky with her daughter Juliet Lashinsky-Revene. The detail shows part of Lashinsky's collection of period family portraits, frames and mirrors. *Opposite:* a view across the central atrium, showing the entrance to Juliet's bedroom suite on the ground floor and Karen's on the second floor. The bronze Art Deco lantern was probably originally hung in a public space. *Right:* detail show-ing the scale of the interior courtyard. *Below:* Janet Brewster painted the ceiling with a motif of cupids on a dark blue night sky. *Below right:* the fireplace was constructed out of new and salvaged materials by Michael Hord and David Ng, and the concrete distressed with coffee, tea, mustard and grease.

On these pages: views of the kitchen. *Above:* a detail of the scullery, which was inspired by a marble dairy in a Scottish ancestral home. The areas of the kitchen designed for food preparation, top, and dining, right, have a more Provençal feel. Many of the elements seen here, including the ladder and much of the cabinetry, were in the building when Lashinsky bought it; she simply adapted them to new uses. The flowers are from David Browne at The Flower Shop, Lashinsky's favourite florist; the country-style chairs were found in a junk store in Maine. The cabinet, right, was found at the flea market on 26th Street, while the flamboyant Empire couch came from a yard sale in upstate New York.

Above: the sun terrace, just off Lashinsky's rooftop garden, was recently decorated in the spirit of an early twentieth-century ocean liner. The Chinese workers who did the renovation also made the wrought-iron doors and window grilles. The wall sconces, which were bought in Amsterdam, provided the original inspiration for this charming corner. *Left:* the small guest room appears to have come straight out of an Agatha Christie novel. The bed, built by John Briggs, folds out from one of the walls in the tiny library, and is disguised by having a row of book spines pasted on its underside. *Opposite:* a view of the master bedroom, where the decor is reminiscent of a turn-of-the-century actress's boudoir.

This very private corner apartment, in a classic 1923 building, is drenched with light. On sunny days the all-ivory colour scheme bounces the luminosity off all the surfaces until it become a box of soft, glowing blondness. Against the pale walls and furnishings the graphic shapes of a fine collection of American folk art stand out sharply. It is a grown-up sort of interior, extremely personal and reflecting the newly independent lives of Susan and Jerry Lauren now that their children have grown up. Prior to moving here they had lived in the same East 66th Street building ever since getting married, simply moving apartments within it to accommodate their growing family. What attracted them to this landmark building was the fact that the area was protected from any additional construction. 'The neighbourhood has a kind of European feel; sometimes it's almost like being in Paris what with all the embassies and the two churches across the street. This is real early Manhattan architecture. The patina on the roofs is actually very similar to the patina on the weathervanes that we collect. We felt that that, in itself, was rather exciting: to look

14

around from inside, and see the windows framing the kind of texture we are most interested in collecting. Even the windows here are made of old glass, so everything seemed to lend itself to what we are about and what we like to collect. That's ultimately what made us take the decision to buy it.' In decorative terms, the apartment is more about what has been left out than what has been included, about the remarkable restraint involved in not hanging pictures, adding throws or introducing colour – a brave stance on the part of Susan. It is this sparing use of texture, colour and furniture that gives the interior its elegance and its impact, and allows it to remain essentially a foil for their collections. The passionate interest that Susan and Jerry Lauren have for folk sculpture has been cultivated slowly over the years. As brother to Ralph Lauren and Director of Men's Design at Polo Ralph Lauren, Jerry Lauren is well placed to collect this kind of art. Yet the couple have been exacting to the point of refusing many 'almost good

enough' pieces, and will willingly travel right across the country in pursuit of others. Their interest began with a little weekend shopping at country auctions; they soon became hooked, learning along the way, making new discoveries and trying to distinguish 'weathervanes that are run-of-the-mill from those that are art: those which have aged and show the patina of time.' The result is a vibrant assembly of objects that have a hundred years of living history. The Laurens' selection is not about value or rarity; rather it is about loving something for itself, for the life it has lived. Thoughtfully unencumbered by an overbearing decor, their collection stands out beautifully in its glorious Park Avenue frame.

Susan & Jerry Lauren

On the opening pages: a portrait of Susan and Jerry Lauren, with pieces from their collection of antique toys. The detail shows one of their nineteenth-century weathervanes. *On these pages:* more pieces from the Laurens' weathervane collection, displayed in the living and dining rooms. The coffee table, opposite, and the dining table, above, are variations on pieces from the Ralph Lauren home collection. The Weissenhof No.MR10 dining chairs, above, are re-editions of a classic 1927 design by Mies van der Rohe.

Jonathan Leitersdorf moved to New York because he wanted to build skyscrapers. His stunning penthouse apartment with its arresting views – towards Lower Manhattan to the south and Midtown to the north – is certainly a stimulating place whence to study his now-favourite city's skyline. There are certainly plenty of fine spots for contemplation: the real lawn that floats high above the city; the stone benches in the English-style garden; the highest terrace of all, with its ergonomic, inclined sun deck; the glassed-in studio room, with its mounds of cushions; and a personal favourite, the porcelain claw-footed bathtub with its perfect view of the full-sized swimming pool. The sybaritic element to Leitersdorf's design for the striking interior of his Broadway penthouse is perhaps in part due to the young architect's Israeli roots. In the Middle East, proper importance is given to the pleasure principle and Leitersdorf obviously places the enjoyment of his interior very high on his list of priorities. 'It's about spaces and activities,' he says. 'When I design, I start with the activity I want to be involved in, then I move on to finding an

architectural language that will complement the activity. The house develops from one activity to the next: I try to create a harmony and some kind of sequence from one room to the other. I like the sense of discovery. I don't like everything to be on view immediately when you come in; I prefer to have people explore it.' Discovering the two-storey penthouse is quite an experience: the space, even by New York standards, is huge. As one of the city's most successful loft-conversion specialists, who buys up entire commercial industrial buildings to convert them to residential use, Leitersdorf was not fazed by the question of scale. He has not attempted to downplay the volume of the place, but rather exploited it for maximum effect. Downstairs, the central space is the lounge-cum-billiard room with a fine dark-wood staircase and the original embossed, slightly arched ceilings, which have been painted silver. Adjacent is a handsome kitchen–dining room and a giant master bedroom, its brick-built walls on view. Leitersdorf has filled the bedroom with old shop fittings, in oak, to house his clothes. Through a carved Indian door lies the master bathroom, in marble, a theatrical chamber which evokes the most modern and minimal of oriental hamans. Upstairs are guest rooms, a relaxation room with huge cushions, glass walls and a view over the lawn, and the swimming pool. An office, further guest rooms and a butler's pantry-style kitchen have been neatly slotted in. It is a true architect's home, designed for maximum impact yet extremely practical despite its grandiose features. What makes it decidedly a home rather than a show house is the prodigious quantity of anecdotal, individual and eccentric furnishings and details. 'I go to flea markets and crazy little antique stores and just buy objects that I like and put them in the space. The energy of the old stuff kind of rubs off on you.'

Jonathan Leitersdorf

On the opening pages: a portrait of Jonathan Leitersdorf on his rooftop lawn. The detail shows a cement bench on a peaceful walkway in the garden, with the Twin Towers looming behind. The antique, hand-embroidered cushions were bought in India. *On this page:* two views of the impressive pool deck. The setting of the swimming pool is quite extraordinary, giving incredible views over the East Village, SoHo and Downtown. *Opposite:* one of the guest bathrooms looks out over the pool. The tub is an early twentieth-century high-backed slipper bath. The taps and shower fixtures are of brass, made to a Victorian design, and the carpet is from Morocco.

Opposite: architect Jonathan Leitersdorf's sprawling bedroom. The brick walls and domed roof have been left raw, and evoke the building's past as a warehouse. *Below:* the elaborately carved door was imported from India, where Leitersdorf has travelled widely. It frames the entrance to a large, luxurious bathroom entirely fitted out in marble and evocative of Arabian hamans. *Right:* these nineteenth-century shop fittings are just part of a treasure-trove of objects which Leitersdorf has brought back from flea markets and antique shops all over the world. Adapted for use as closets and shelving, they are displayed in a sunny corner of the huge bedroom. The vintage leather club armchairs, bought in Paris, contribute to the masculine atmosphere.

Left: the antique dining table in a windowed alcove off the kitchen. *Below:* the living room is mostly used as a games room. The pool table and lamp are ornate antique finds, as is the bar. The mouldings on the ceiling were in place when Leitersdorf bought the space, and were probably an early twentieth-century embellishment. Painted silver, they now give a modern edge to the room. *Opposite:* the blue marble kitchen has been beautifully designed with both high-tech cooking appliances and junk shop finds, such as the handsome brass light fitting.

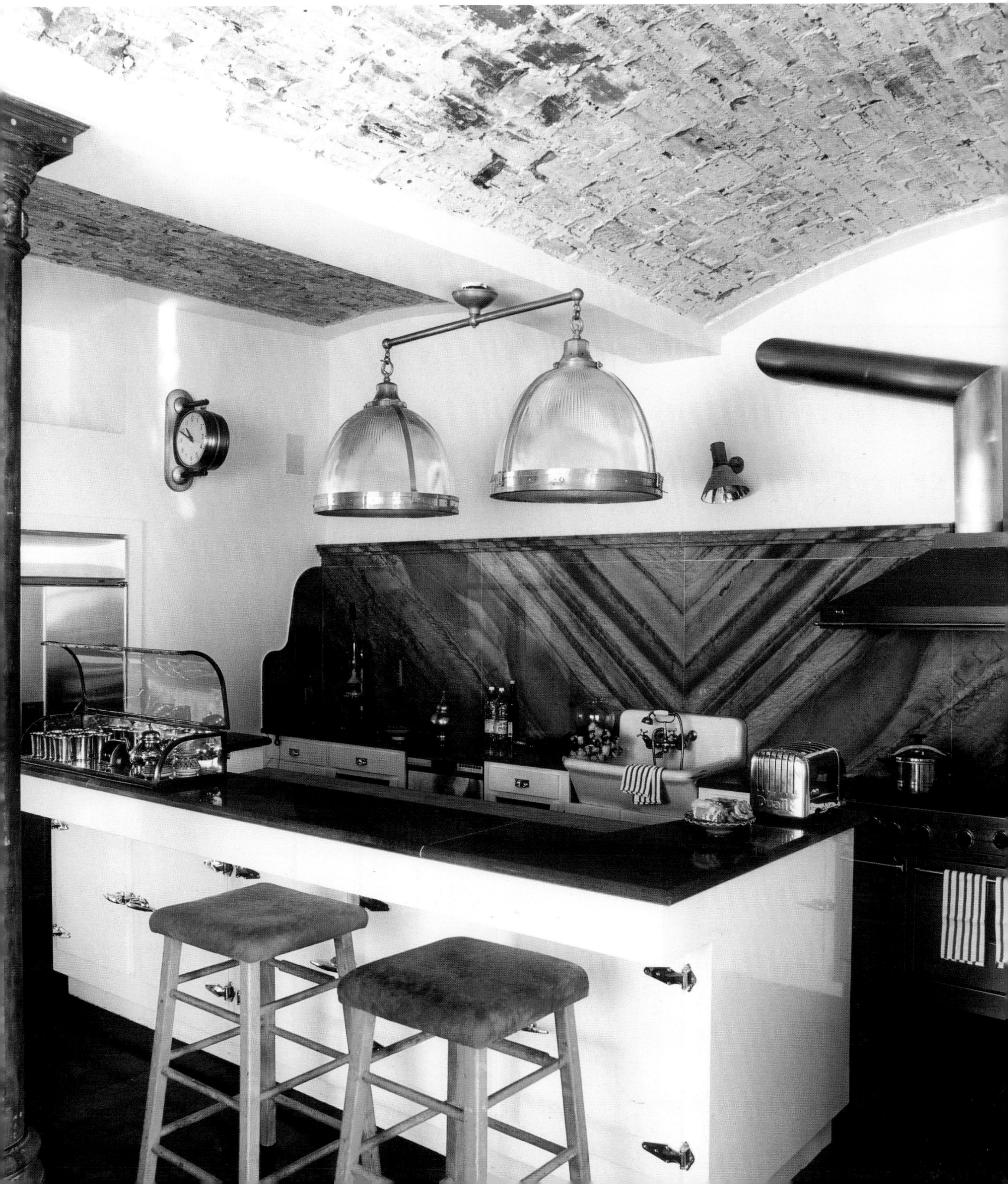

Marian McEvoy is plainly a powerful woman, but she is also a romantic – as is evident from one look at her shell-studded apartment. She lives fast as the high-flying Editor of one of America's best-known interiors magazines and yet, since moving into this luscious pale yellow space, she has enjoyed nothing more than spending afternoons with a hot glue gun and 300-pound bags of shells imported from India. What is more, McEvoy, who seems the consummate New Yorker, is West Coast-born and Paris bred – aesthetically at least, because that is where she truly spread her wings as a journalist, married, and generally became *au fait* with style in all its seductive forms. It was her familiarity with fashion in particular that was significant in her approach to *Elle Decor*, the magazine she has run since its beginnings in 1991. She came to it straight from Paris, being 'more excited by sofas than sweaters'. She recalls the move: 'It was a bit of a shock. Achievement and money are extremely important here, whereas in France it was more about having a marvellous time. Aesthetics, though, were written with a capital A.' McEvoy first lived in a SoHo loft –

'a perfect cube and such a delicious space to live in' – but the accelerated gentrification of the area became something of a pressure. ('Every time I came back at night, dozens of people would wave at me from the restaurants,' she recalls). She regretfully decided that the time had come to do the grown-up thing and buy a place of her own, even if it had to be in a less fashionable neighbourhood. In fact, her apartment is in a chaotic slice of Midtown, near her office and just across from the loading bay of Bloomingdales department store. She likes this view, since the grand old shop's gables and leaded roofs remind her of Paris. When she settled on this 1865 space, principally seduced by the back-to-back fireplace that had been created by combining two apartments, there was no option but to transform it completely. 'It was a wreck. I do not like perfect things – I am un-American in that way, I don't care if things aren't neat and polished and pristine. I like a bit of wear and tear, and this definitely had it.' She ripped down walls, re-did the plumbing and turned the three tiny bedrooms into one, with an en-suite boudoir, and painted it a 'deep, dirty, dusty blue, which is very soothing'. The main space became a yellow canvas for her shell-sticking activities. 'I have

always lived with yellow, I guess because in Paris it is so grey all the time.' She also remodelled the doorways, taking them up to the ceiling – 'an inexpensive trick that always works to improve the proportions'. Thankfully, her walls are the original period plaster, and not the characterless sheet rock that she so dislikes; the uneven texture of the plaster is the perfect background for her delicate patterns. 'In the country I do similar collages with feathers and pine cones. I always like to have little elements of nature around me – after all, the best things in life are free!'

Marian McEvoy

On the opening pages: a portrait of Marian McEvoy at home in her Midtown apartment. The detail shows one of her seashell collages. *On the previous double page:* the living room, showing the stately double-sided fireplace that lured McEvoy into buying the apartment. The colour scheme in this room is mostly black and white, dramatically set off by the pale yellow walls. The mirror above the fireplace is by Maite Dubois and Claire Cormier-Fauvel. *Opposite:* a huge shell forms the centrepiece for the dining table. *Above:* at the other end of the apartment, a French nineteenth-century bed has been upholstered in black and painted white; it is now used as a sofa. Marian McEvoy created the black shell frame of the mirror above it.

Left: a detail of the delicate shellwork on the frames surrounding the classical casement windows. *Below:* a corner of the dining room, with a definite oriental feel. The wrought-iron chair was a flea market find. *Opposite:* Marian McEvoy's striking bedroom. She created the bedhead and screens using ribbons and shells, and also embellished the pair of mirrors that hang either side of the bed. The Chinese-made white cotton embroidered bedspread was found in a discount catalogue.

One of the most unexpected spaces in New York, artist Izhar Patkin's place is a mind-blowing hybrid of laboratory, studio and sprawling domestic interior. Like his art, it perfectly expresses his talent for transforming prosaic elements into something sublime. Patkin is at home with the magical: this century-old school house has become a maze of brightly coloured, highly seductive rooms. It is a true artist's interior, not only because of its unusually large spaces – three interior courtyards, a massive terrace and a labyrinth of rooms, all dotted with his large-scale mixed-media canvases and sculpture – but also because it expresses a completely original way of looking at things. References to myth and legend are implicit in Patkin's work; likewise in his home, different rooms express different levels of consciousness. Much of this, he says, comes from his own heritage. 'My family was one of the pioneering families in Israel. Stories are an important part of our culture: stories about how the country was built, about the family's Russian past. It was all about legacy, about direct impact upon a small environment. Then I moved to America,

17

this vast place where I felt a great loss of familiarity. My art was a way of bridging this gap; it had to do with the transformation of stories and the loss of intimacy.' Israeli-born but trained in New York, Patkin also learned to be inventive about the way he lived: among his first pads in the big city was the converted lobby of a Chelsea building. Today, however, he has the space to do practically whatever he wants, and in his new East Village location he has allowed his imagination to run riot. None of the rooms has a designated role. 'I don't see things as static. What is nice about this place is the *passage*, how you go from one room to the other. In the Middle East when you walk around the old markets and cities, the *passage* becomes your main experience. I also appreciate being on the ground floor because I like the sense of outside and inside merging – not only in terms of the courtyards, but also in terms of the street. I find it intriguing to be at the same level as the street; it's an effortless way of being in touch with the neighbourhood, which is very important to me.' His approach is bi-cultural: the ease and modernity of America is crossed with the sensuality and theatricality of the Levant. Patkin's interior also precisely reflects his approach to art. 'My work is always about constructing a good story – a narrative and everything that forms it. You choose the right materials and technique for that particular story and they become part of your narrative. They are chosen according to what might make the story more complex and seductive. Most of the work I do stems from wanting to see things that I haven't seen before, and a lot of that translated into the house. The important thing is that I came to this place as a painter and sculptor, not as a designer. The decisions were made in the same way as if I were making a sculpture, but since the house was not a piece of art I didn't try to make things perfect.'

Izhar Patkin

On the opening pages: a portrait of Izhar Patkin, and a detail of one of the leafy courtyards that link the various old school-house buildings that make up his home. *On the previous double page:* the main courtyard. The chairs are by Harry Bertoia for Knoll; the table is in fact a Moroccan tray on metal legs. *Above:* the same courtyard seen from another angle. *Opposite above:* the studio where Patkin works on his cutouts, collages and works on paper. *Opposite below:* Patkin in the two-level sunken painting studio. The works seen to the left are part of the series called *Gardens for the Global City*.

Above: a view of the kitchen. The dish rack, made by Patkin, is laden with Venetian, American and Mexican glass, as well as pitchers for everyday use. The canvas is by Kim MacConnel. *Opposite:* the mixed-media sculpture, called *Funeral TV*, dates from 1991 and is by Izhar Patkin in collaboration with Nam June Paik. Beyond it can be seen the entrance to the main painting studio. The carpets are Moroccan.

Opposite: the extra-long dining table is central to the char-treuse-painted kitchen space. The lamp, with its coloured glass candle-holders, was bought in a junk shop and came originally from a church. The chairs probably date from the 1940s. *Left:* a view of the table from the hot pink entrance salon. *Below:* the couch was designed by Kim MacConnel, 'about thirty years ago'. Some of the cushions are made from velvet designed by Patkin for Romeo Gigli; others are silk-screen designs by Salvador de Bahia's homeless children. The pictures are by Kim MacConnel, Jean-Michel Basquiat, Nam June Paik and Izhar Patkin. The chairs were painted by Kim MacConnel, and the table is Moroccan.

On these pages: Patkin's charming dressing room, above, features several layers of Moroccan tribal carpets and a Turkish chandelier in red glass. The curtains concealing the shelves are made from tinsel-embroidered Indian fabric, which would more usually be worn as a wedding sari. Two of Patkin's sculptures can be found in the office-cum-library, seen through the door and in the picture opposite. The life-size equestrian sculpture, cast in polychromatic anodized aluminium, is entitled *Don Quixote Segunda Parte*.

Opposite: a view of the bright blue-painted bathroom, which has been left unplastered. A Turkish chandelier in blue glass hangs from the skylight. *Left:* a detail of Izhar Patkin's hot tub, in tinted cement, which has been treated with salt especially imported from the Dead Sea. *Above:* Patkin's bedroom; his bed comprises several mattresses piled on top of each other, in the oriental style. The bold green striped curtains were hand-painted by Patkin; he also created the lamp, which is made from plastic lanterns bought during a trip to India.

When Doris Lockhart Saatchi was a child her parents sometimes took her to New York for day trips. For the little girl – who must have been incubating what was to blossom into her remarkably acute sense of aesthetics – the big city was paradise. The theatre, the shops, the sophistication of it all overwhelmed her, and excited her. One day, she promised herself, 'I will live in New York'. So, years later – by which time she had become a collector, devoted disciple of minimalism, editor and internationally respected art consultant – when she first visited this nineteenth-century row house it was the beginning of a complex process that was to make her dream come true. In the East 50s, the area around the United Nations that is studded with embassies, the house was quiet and enjoyed an unexpectedly generous view of the river. Despite the fact that the building as it then stood did not reach her exacting architectural standards, she bought three derelict floors of it, realizing its potential even though it was terribly run down and had unexciting proportions. The state of the place was such that before any kind of design could be conceived it had to

be gutted. Saatchi, rich in experience from working with English minimalists Claudio Silvestrin and especially the high priest of the genre, John Pawson, felt strongly that although she had very defined ideas about what she wanted, she did need an ally. Enter William Fellows, a young and enthusiastic architect without much of a background in minimalism but understandably flattered and stimulated by the prospect of working with such a interesting client. It proved to be a perfect combination. Today the house is a breathtaking exercise in purity, a luminous backdrop for the conceptual works that Saatchi collects and a monument to her clarity of vision in its own right. Everything, right down to the taps and cupboard doors, has been specially designed. It is, no doubt, this minute attention to detail that makes the space such an elegant experience. When one walks through the door and first inspects the interior, however, it is the dramatic architectural gestures that register, and that overwhelm the eye and the senses, giving the lasting impression of an exceptional space. Such a strong statement is rare in the context of a domestic interior. Saatchi and Fellows have created a double-height drawing room with a sheet of glass as a window-wall; tall narrow passageways that contrast with the generous, wide open spaces; a mezzanine office with bird's-eye views; and a bedroom that appears to float directly above the East River. All this has been accomplished as a kind of conceptual geometric puzzle involving forms, textures, the play of light and a million shades of white; it is a design of uncommon complexity. Saatchi's emotional involvement in the house is palpable. Like the Sol LeWitt sculpture in the garden, *Incomplete Open Cube*, which curiously reflects the architecture, the home appears to be a visual rendering of someone's soul. There is little for Saatchi to say, this close to perfection, except, smiling: 'This is as near as can be to my dream house.'

Doris Lockhart Saatchi

On the opening pages: the dining room table on the ground floor of Doris Lockhart Saatchi's triplex. The table was designed by Saatchi and, as elsewhere in the house, uses sustainable, farmed wood. The chairs are by Harry Bertoia for Knoll. Opposite is a view of the main space looking towards the garden; the sculpture is by Sol LeWitt. *On these pages:* two views of the main living space. The leather sofas are reproductions of designs by Josef Hoffman. The painting over the fireplace, by Tim Rollins and к.о.s., is called *The Whiteness of the Whale* and is composed of pages from *Moby Dick* pasted onto a canvas and then painted over.

Left: the bedroom. The bed was made to a design by Doris Saatchi. *Below:* a painting by Ian Davenport, 6.7 metres (22 feet) long, dominates the mezzanine office. The lamp is a silver-plated re-edition of a Bauhaus design. Doris Saatchi designed the marble desk, and the small collage is by Stephen Buckley. The floor, as elsewhere in the house, is in Italian *pietra serena. Opposite:* the chair in the foreground is by Garouste and Bonetti and the ceramic vase is by Peter Slesinger. The white Carrara marble basin, just visible behind the partition, was designed by Doris Saatchi.

Scale has always been an issue for artist Julian Schnabel. Volume, proportions, weight … he consistently and unrepentantly thinks big. His famous plate pictures routinely weighed a ton, and his canvases sometimes have the proportions of theatre backgrounds. It is hardly surprising, therefore, that the Manhattan home he shares with his wife Olatz and their twins Cy and Olmo should be monumental, lofty and vast. A converted perfume factory, it is as gritty and intense as his pictures, with much of the raw industrial finishing left visible. The artworks themselves are everywhere, and are so big that they sometimes appear as walls of velvety, richly pigmented and stained canvas. The overwhelming visual impact of their home is such that one is forced to confront all kinds of questions: is the building just an outsized frame for the pictures that hang there, is it part of the art itself, or is daily life here just an extension of the painting? With Schnabel you simply never know, because his art is so all encompassing, and inseparable from the man himself. Decoration, architectural design and furniture making are chief among his extracurricular

19

interests. He thus distances himself from the small-minded and specifically twentieth-century fear of being termed decorative, a label most artists despise. Speaking to him, however, all conceptual theories are brushed aside: for Schnabel, his home is nothing if not an integral part of a love story, every inch of it designed and made together with his beautiful Basque wife Olatz after she finally agreed to marry him. Following an extended courtship, during which he painted a series of giant canvases with her name inscribed across them, Olatz moved to New York from Europe and they decided to rehabilitate the building – in which Schnabel already lived – in order to build their home. Together they completely transformed the raw second floor below his studio, turning five massive rooms into an exceptional domestic interior. His talent for furniture making and her interest in textiles, colours and textures – she is a designer of fine linens – has led to the unconventional juxtaposition of unplastered walls with rich velvet hangings, antiques and colossal pieces of art; the result is 'like a pirate's idea of heaven'. Schnabel built a big rolled steel sleigh bed for his wife, and she covered it with embroidered linens that look as though they were made in Cuba during the last century. They then smashed

a hole in the wall in front of the bed, so the morning view would open to the gardens and the backs of the houses in the West Village. They also installed an antique marble bathtub in the middle of the giant bedroom so that he could watch her having her bath, while she could look at the paintings. They are comfortable being dwarfed by the scale of the place, with its cathedral-sized doorways and monumental proportions, and feel that they 'live in a time warp somewhere between the set of Cocteau's *Les Enfants Terribles* and a seventeenth-century Spanish feudal manor'.

Olatz & Julian Schnabel

On the opening pages: a snapshot of Julian and Olatz Schnabel, with their twins and Schnabel's daughter Lola in the background. The detail shows a corner of Schnabel's vast New York studio, in a nineteenth-century perfume factory. *Left:* a view of the kitchen with its soaring ceiling. The paintings are by Schnabel: on the left is *E. Oen*, 1988, and on the right *Matelda (Map of Heaven and Hell)*, also 1988. The dining table was also designed by Schnabel. *Below:* another view of the dining table showing the textured surface which Schnabel created with multicoloured cement tiles from Europe.

Opposite: a seventeenth-century Flemish tapestry hangs in the vast living room. The side tables are Biedermeier, and the hippopotamus skull is nineteenth-century. The paintings form part of a series called *Los Patos del Buen Retiro*, 1991. *Below:* a monumental bronze sculpture, *Leutwyler for BB*, 1989–90; the painting in the background is *Untitled (Zeus)*, 1992. The doors on the right, which lead to the living room, were the original entrance doors into the factory.

Above: Julian Schnabel's painting *Olatz*, 1991, part of the series the artist painted when he was courting his Basque wife. *Above left:* a view of the twins' bathroom showing a portrait of their mother by George Condo. *Right:* a large painting by Francesco Clemente hangs in the children's bedroom. The miniature children's furniture in the foreground is antique. The sleigh bed, in burl wood, is French Empire. The pale green embroidered bed linen was designed by Olatz Schnabel and handmade in her home town of San Sebastian.

Left: a view of the master bedroom showing an Aubusson carpet and a Syrie Maugham sleigh bed upholstered in red velvet; the bed used to belong to Stephen Tennant. The painting behind it is *Eulalio Epiclantos, After Seeing St Jean Vianney on the Plains of the Cure d'Ars*, 1986. The large painting is *Teddy Bears Picnic*, 1987. The bath in the foreground is Roman, acquired in Puerto Rico. *Below:* Schnabel made the rolled iron sleigh bed himself; the linen sheets were designed by Olatz. She also created the curtains, which are put together from antique velvet and old bedspreads.

David Seidner is one of the very few photographers whose work successfully straddles the worlds of fine art and commercial fashion. Seidner was born in Los Angeles but subsequently based himself in Paris and now New York. While one facet of his work has been exhibited extensively in galleries and museums, the other has been published in many of the best magazines. This is something of a rarity in contemporary creative circles, where people love to categorize and separate 'true' creators from those who merely 'design' images for the voracious world of fashion. Seidner's home in SoHo similarly expresses an apparent contradiction. On the one hand, he is drawn to the ideal of the 'millennial urge to streamline': a sensual minimalism is much in evidence, as can be seen in his fondness for the smooth lines and understated curves of Scandinavian pottery and the furniture of Jean-Michel Frank. On the other hand, his home has the cheerful incongruity of a born collector's accumulations, the whimsical spoils that come with succumbing to the seduction of the flea markets of Paris. Seidner's transcontinental existence has almost

20

inevitably resulted in a tendency towards amassing and assembling, so his pared-down home is nonetheless very far removed from the sterile environment of true minimalists. Articulate, cultivated and generous, Seidner evolved among fellow artists with whom to swap works was a natural process. This has led to a rare collection of contemporary art: portraits, works on paper, canvases by friends or of friends. He also has an endearing and irrational fondness for quirky, characterful things, such as a 1940s cement table and a wooden tromp l'œil chair. Likewise, although the converted workshop space in which he lives is a triumph of purist proportions and muted tones, the odd stain of misty red upholstery, the unpredictable nature of the ethnic artefacts, the textures and the art itself give the place a more individual spirit. The space is the product of what Seidner calls a 'kamikaze restoration'. It took him precisely four weeks to turn what had at various times been a cult's headquarters, a hippie crash-out and an art gallery into a perfectly compartmentalized home and work environment. The office and studio are at street level, and the kitchen acts as a natural divider between them and Seidner's domestic space. His private quarters are accessed through a narrow passageway. The soaring ceiling and the large, unstructured space have a striking impact. This room for living in, with its mezzanine bedroom, is almost a perfect square. The original crumbling skylight, which has now been perfectly restored, infuses it with soft but steady filtered light. Seidner stripped the floor, reorganized the structure of the place and then left the industrial brick of the nineteenth-century walls apparent, thinly veiled under a coat of white matt paint. He has transformed the place into a refuge, a soothing foil for his collections, expressing his particular doctrine of 'organic modernism, with no hard edges'. David Seidner's images all share a rare purity, an idealized force that makes them memorable, and his home is without doubt the three-dimensional expression of his very particular eye.

David Seidner

On the opening pages: a self-portrait by David Seidner, and a general view of his atelier space in SoHo. *Below:* a Knoll sideboard props up a painting by Suzanne McClelland. The other works are by Ross Bleckner, Terry Winters and Philip Taaffe. *Right:* the dining area features a table designed by Frank Lloyd Wright. The chairs are 1930s French. The plaster floor lamp was designed and made by Seidner; the string lamp is by George Jense. The ceramics include pieces by Rörstrand, Fantoni and Royal Copenhagen.

Opposite: the loft space has been left in its original raw state, with the pipes visible and the texture of the bricks clearly apparent through the whitewash. The highly sophisticated finishes on the 1950s furniture contrast pleasingly with this roughness. Covering the bed are Calvin Klein linens and a James Gould mohair blanket. The sidetables are by Frank Lloyd Wright. *Above:* a couch by Knoll and two Parisian elm-trunk chairs sit in the entrance to the apartment. *Right:* Seidner has an extensive collection of artworks by friends and contemporaries, much of it on view in this corner of the bedroom. The watercolour portrait of David seen at the bottom right is by Francesco Clemente.

The colourful interiors of this beautifully put-together apartment do not immediately suggest urban living, let alone the traditional strait-laced style of the Upper East Side. As you walk through the door into the pale yellow entrance hall, with its brightly coloured French cement-tile floor, the atmosphere recalls the relaxed pace of the Mediterranean. Surely only an expert stylist could have achieved such an instinctive response. Indeed, this is the home of journalist and editor Suzanne Slesin, Design Editor at *House & Garden* magazine and a past master at the art of creating a suggestive environment. As a writer she is internationally renowned for her series of style books which completely revolutionized the field of interiors publishing, paving the way for subsequent works such as this one. As a design guru she has travelled widely in search of the world's most interesting architecture and decor, all of which has left a mark on her taste. Naturally enough, this is reflected in her home, a large Park Avenue apartment which she shares with her husband Michael Steinberg, an art dealer and writer, and their two teenage children. The

21

apartment is only a few blocks away from the family's previous New York home, which they lived in for eighteen years. It was a wreck when Slesin discovered it, and had a labyrinth of 'unused maids' rooms and hideous bathrooms with acres of corridor,' she recalls. 'What appealed to us was that no one had done anything to it, so it was a blank slate.' The family actually had to have half of it rebuilt, with the help of the French architectural designer Jean-Louis Ménard. 'We wanted to do something that related to the fact that it was a traditional, old-fashioned Park Avenue building. We had to fight the temptation to make the kitchen bigger than the living room, and more central, which would have suited our lifestyle but probably not the apartment. We followed Ménard's advice and just redistributed the space.' This was an inspired idea: although it has not been promoted to taking over one of the street-side reception rooms, the enlarged kitchen has evolved into being the real heart of the house. The dark space it previously occupied has now been reworked to make an Aladdin's cave of a larder and pantry. It is stocked with much of the charming bric-a-brac that the couple have brought back from their travels and antique-hunting, such as painted biscuit tins, woven baskets, wire utensils, rustic crockery and colourful china. The formal dining room, which might well have remained the least lived-in room of the house, was rescued by being turned into a much-needed library. Its dark, leaf-green *boiseries* and perfect proportions, together with the overflowing piles of books, make it

instantly appealing. Throughout the house are scattered a multitude of unusual objects and paintings. Slesin has a great eye, and traces of her passion for rustic or little-known domestic artefacts can be seen everywhere – each piece has some special merit which warrants it being included in her highly selective collection. Indeed, she likes to describe her comfortable idiosyncratic home as nothing more than 'a lot of collections, and very little furniture'.

Suzanne Slesin & Michael Steinberg

On the opening pages: a portrait of Suzanne Slesin and Michael Steinberg's two children, and a detail of the wire lamp in the living room. *Above:* part of the entrance to their apartment, showing the brightly coloured cement floortiles by the French company Carocim. The small tin flowers have been collected from around the world and were probably used in cemeteries. *Left:* the kitchen. The chairs were designed by friends Jean-Louis Ménard and Daniel Rozensztroch, for a company in Greece. The distinctive wooden sign, 'Café au Chez-Nous', is probably Canadian, and was bought at an antique fair. *On the following double page:* the library, designed by Jean-Louis Ménard. The lamp was originally intended for a pool table.

Opposite: the piano originally belonged to Suzanne Slesin's mother. The unusual four-tiered vase probably came originally from a florist's display. In the foreground, the occasional table with chessboard motif is American country. *Above:* the painting above the fireplace is by Keith Haring. The coffee table is made from an old piece of marble and sections of a balustrade. The felt carpet was bought in Istanbul, and is most likely a Turkish tribal piece. The consoles are French, and the paintings above them are nineteenth-century.

Above: a view of the master bedroom; the green and white bathroom can also be seen through the open door. The elaborately painted chest of drawers and bed are part of a 1940s set of cottage furniture. The wardrobe was bought in an antique store on Long Island, while the patchwork quilt is part of Slesin and Steinberg's collection of such pieces. The ornate wood frame on top of the wardrobe is a piece of ingenious salvage art bought in New York. *Opposite:* facing the bed is an untitled 1976 painting by the Swiss artist Gregoire Mueller. The chair is by Garouste and Bonetti; the lamp was bought from a flower shop and is probably 1940s.

As the elevator rises up to the Upper East Side apartment of art gallery owner Holly Solomon, one cannot help wondering how her well-known collection of cutting-edge contemporary art will look in the reduced proportions of this typically 1920s apartment block. Solomon moved here in December 1997 from a large apartment in Sutton Place where she had lived for thirty years and 'which was about a family situation, about entertaining children, small parties, huge parties …' Much of the activity at Sutton Place had begun when she became one of the key figures (first as a collector and later as a dealer) in the alternative art movement of the late 1960s and early 70s. Driven by her free spirit and her quick, generous mind, Solomon's first trail-blazing SoHo gallery represented a new current that was later to transform the New York art world through the introduction of multi-media conceptual installation and alternative art forms. 'It was not about exclusivity,' Solomon says of that time. 'It was about innovation and a dialogue within the art community: we did poetry readings, performances, films – it was breathtaking. Our real concern was with the

22

role that the gallery plays in society, which should be community-oriented and culturally responsible.' Solomon was an innovator in her choice of artists, her choice of location – she was one of the first to embrace the SoHo reconversion movement – and her remarkable attitude: she continues to have more of the mentor than the merchant about her. It is this approach that has carried her eponymous gallery through the roller-coaster economics of the art world over the last two-and-a-half decades, and allowed it to emerge with its reputation intact. In 1988 Solomon wrote a book called *Living with Art*, wherein she evoked 'the creation of a personally satisfying home that combines art and decor – a place that somehow, often quite magically, adds up to more than the sum of its individual parts.' In the case of her new one-bedroomed pad the individual parts are, on the one side, modest proportions seemingly enlarged by a bold use of colour (candy-floss pink for the dining room, lime green for the corridor and deep baby blue for the living room) and on the other, a spectacular and very personal choice of movable and ever-changing art. There are canvases by Warhol, Wegman, Christo and Rauschenberg, among others, while the surfaces of the walls themselves have been painted by Kim MacConnel and Jean Lowe. 'Theirs is a very personal point of view – when I walk through the door I always smile because I feel their presence. But I also feel mine, because great artists know how to share – they include their audience. It's really a fantasy house, but it's also about love. When I walk in I think, Yes, my life has really been decent.' Although Solomon admits that 'moving to the Upper East Side is like moving to another country,' she has made the apartment so much a part of her personal landscape that it screams out evidence of her energy, her unquenchable curiosity and her pioneering spirit. 'It is all about being mature,' she says with a twinkle in her eye, curled up in her armchair with cigarette in hand *à la* Greta Garbo. 'That, and wanting to live a dignified but cosy life.'

Holly Solomon

On the opening pages: a portrait of Holly Solomon, and a corner of her living room. Over the fireplace is Christo's 'wrapped' 1966 portrait of Solomon in pin-up pose. *On the previous double page:* the living room features a work on fabric by Izhar Patkin, used as a wall hanging, and a six-panel screen print of Solomon by Andy Warhol. The carpet is by Kim MacConnel. The sculpture on the right, entitled *Dog*, is by Nam June Paik. *Opposite:* a partial view of the kitchen, which is decorated with butterfly wallpaper by Rob Wynne. The painting in the pink dining room, visible through the open door, is by Nam June Paik. *Above:* Holly Solomon's bedroom. The painted armchair and the picture over the bed are by Kim MacConnel.

Row upon endless row of books: that is what first strikes you about Jane Stubbs' interior. Books on art, architecture, the decorative arts, fashion and gardening; new books, old books, even extremely rare and antiquarian books – all are the welcome legacy of Stubbs' celebrated gallery of collector's volumes and works on paper. Now that she works with New York's Municipal Art Society the books have come to rest here, in these pink, blue and green rooms that look as though they might have come straight from her native Natchez, Mississippi. Stubbs' East Village apartment has been entirely decorated with family heirlooms, most of them in deep auburn cherrywood and maple, which evoke the Deep South of the mid-nineteenth century. Indeed, the furniture could previously be found in the gracious plantation house in which Stubbs grew up. 'Collecting seems to be in the family: I am an incurable hoarder, as was my mother. Her great-aunt, from whom she inherited all this stuff, even had boxes of notepads and scratch paper from 1870 that nobody knows what to do with. It is not interesting, it is just trash. We have lots of that.'

23

But a trashy interior this is not: it is more of a trip into the America of Henry James, with added Southern flavour, delicately overlaid with layers of Stubbs' own contemporary sophistication. With a little decorative sleight of hand and a highly individual sense of proportion these blue-blooded heirlooms have been slotted into an urban space – where the scale of the rooms is most unlike Natchez circa 1840. Not that it feels like New York: the pale green sitting room is like nothing so much as an English nineteenth-century parlour gone mad. Then there is an idiosyncratic library-cum-dining room and a slightly more contained bedroom – with walls that mutate, according to the light, from petrol to baby blue – dominated by a huge colonial-type bed in cherrywood, complete with crocheted hangings. 'It's country Sheraton, probably inspired by rather high-style English things but interpreted through very provincial eyes. There were always four-poster beds in plantation houses. It has been my bed all my life, except for a few years when I was married.' From the bedroom, one steps straight out into what appears to be a luxurious tree house. This exceptional deck has been painted with what looks like Chinese lacquer but is in fact nothing more than plain and effective fireman-red paint. The contrast with the tender green of the leaves (Stubbs' terrace is situated at just the right height to give the illusion that one is actually perched in the branches) is theatrical and quite beautiful. It is one of the main reasons why Stubbs took the apartment. 'It was a frightful mess otherwise, but exactly what I had wanted for so long, a little 1860s brownstone in the East Village. This is what I've aspired to all the years I've been in the city, especially after living in a loft which of course, being me, was hardly a nice minimal spare space – it was so full of stuff!'

Jane Stubbs

On the opening pages: a portrait of Jane Stubbs on her terrace, and the tree-height wooden 'deck' which overlooks her East Village neighbours. Some of the cushions have been specially made but most were picked up on her travels. *Opposite:* two details of her living room, which is a shrine to Vesuvius and the volcano-lovers of the late eighteenth and early nineteenth century such as Sir William Hamilton. The many images were bought all over the world, some of them – such as the large photograph – sourced by friends (in this case Hamish Bowles) who know of her unusual collection. *Below:* the table in the dining room-cum-library is covered in yellow silk. The portraits are mostly family heirlooms.

Opposite: Jane Stubbs' cherrywood bed, which she has slept in almost continuously since childhood, hails from the family home at Natchez. The painting on the left is a mid-nineteenth-century gouache, described by Stubbs as 'a romantic and eccentric bouquet'. The toy rabbit, dressed in a velvet outfit, is nineteenth-century. The canopy over the bed was inherited from Stubbs' great-aunt; Stubbs thinks it was probably 'a colonial revival substitute for the original really big curtains'. *Above:* detail of the corridor, with a partial view of the bathroom. The 1940s plaster console was bought at a flea market and the artichoke-shaped tulip vase came from an auction.

The moment you step into Alan Tanksley's studio apartment, you are aloft in the New York skyline. He has chosen a very glamorous form of one-room living – his space on the seventeenth floor of a 1927 building seems suspended high up among the skyscrapers of Midtown, their gilded cornices and limestone façades twinkling with a thousand lit windows at night. These were originally the trophy headquarters of a pre-Depression life insurance company. Due to the strict classicism of the apartment, with its correct use of proportion, scale and colour, all those glowing windows against the night sky do not seem an invasion; rather, they appear as an alluring backdrop to the domestic scenes played out in Tanksley's cocktail lounge-cum-bedroom. While his view represents one of the great clichés of New York, it is nonetheless still exhilarating. Moreover, the glory of the apartment lies in how Tanksley has managed to create an interior of such intensity that the view does not dominate it, but rather remains a backdrop. Tanksley possesses a very architectural sensibility, and wanted everything to be clean-cut so as not to compete with the active back-

24

ground of the city. His treatment of the apartment has been fairly radical: when the young decorator first visited it seven years ago, shortly before starting his own business, it comprised two small rooms with numerous loft beds and 'wagon-wheel' art. It felt poky, despite the handsome proportions of the windows. He saw its potential immediately and knocked down a wall, making one open space with an enlarged bathroom. Here one can probably have the finest bathing-time view in New York, especially since Tanksley has surrounded the bath with mirrors, thus reflecting the Empire State Building as well as all the other towers. The tiny kitchen is open-plan, and a minuscule sleeping loft above it serves as a spare bedroom. Throughout, Tanksley's approach has been to reintroduce symmetry and to give the room substance by using solid, handsomely proportioned furniture that properly belongs in a much bigger house, therefore lending a sense of permanence and elegance. He has also added a touch of luxury: Tanksley's fine eye has guided him into wisely placing only a few of his possessions while keeping the rest in storage. The result is a triumph of restraint that even he is impressed with. His choice of a dark tobacco tone for the walls may seem unexpected but it is a major contribution to the surprisingly intimate atmosphere. 'It turned out to be the perfect foil for the urban vista that you get through these over-scaled windows. During the day, the darkness of the walls creates great framed pictures: although the buildings are static, the clouds move, the light changes. I am always discovering new things in the cityscape. At night, lighter coloured walls make you feel exposed and more at the mercy of the city, but the dark walls absorb my lighting and let the view expand endlessly beyond the intimate lamp-lit interior.'

Alan Tanksley

On the opening pages: the decorator Alan Tanksley perched precariously on his window ledge, and the view towards some of the finest vintage skyscrapers in midtown Manhattan. *Above:* a detail of his one-room apartment showing a nine-teenth-century Eastern European desk, crafted to a Biedermeier design. The late nineteenth-century painting above it is by an unidentified artist, probably French. On the table to the left is a collection of early twentieth-century machine parts. *Opposite:* the leather and bronze table at the end of the bed is Italian, dating from the 1970s. The painting over the bed is by Stewart Wheeler, and is one of a series of scenes he painted on the New Jersey shore in the 1950s.

Above: a detail of the bathroom. The mahogany cabinet was designed by Tanksley, and the painting is by James Ziegler. The bust is an unidentified 1930s ceramic piece representing the head of a young boy and was bought at one of the antique shows in NYC that Tanksley enjoys attending. *Right:* the bath and shower are ingeniously placed so as to get the most from the spectacular view. The taps and showerhead are contemporary, and the ironwood bowl in the foreground is African. The Gothic-style skyscraper in the background is the New York Life Insurance Building.

Isabel and Ruben Toledo's 'marriage of art and fashion' is a New York byword for that most unusual achievement, a successful union of complementary creative souls. Their life and imaginative talents are so interlinked that the Fashion Institute of Technology staged a well-deserved show around them in 1996, showcasing at the same time her forward-thinking fashion designs and his whimsical, surreal illustrations and paintings. In those hallowed halls their work was displayed in a delicious mix, just as the way it is conceived in this studio-cum-ballroom high above Tin Pan Alley. Her *toiles* and his ink pots and paints coexist, different vehicles for matching talents. As if to reinforce their different modes of expression, their space has two very distinct atmospheres. On the one side is a vast nineteenth-century painter's studio-type area, almost Parisian in feel, its north-facing *atelier* window stretching right up to the roof where it becomes a skylight; and on the other is a high-ceilinged room where, through the many sash windows, one catches glimpses of the façade's fluted grey granite columns, giving a definite neoclassical ambience. Ruben and Isabel, who

are both Cuban émigrés, met in Spanish class as schoolchildren. For Ruben it was love at first sight, and Isabel has remained his muse ever since, her singular profile reappearing time after time in his art. Isabel took a little convincing, but eventually succumbed to his bold good looks, his lively humour and his quick mind. They moved to Manhattan when they got married, in 1984, immediately becoming part of the city's bohemian artistic elite. This is the Toledos' third workspace; they have something of a talent for catching onto neighbourhoods just before they become fashionable. 'This area is now just being discovered. Almost everywhere you look in Manhattan, the spaces have been divided and redone. Around here, all is raw, so you can find great places for a fraction of the price.' Unbelievably, despite the glorious and highly individual architectural characteristics of this particular top-floor eyrie, every light source was covered up when they moved in. ('It was an architects' studio. I think the light must have bothered them.') Isabel and Ruben stripped it down to its original proportions and then let it be, allowing the unusual structure to speak for itself. 'It's a clear space to move around. We didn't set out to create an atmosphere, it just happened. Everything is on wheels so it's totally mobile, everything can be changed. The furniture is all stuff we've had since we were teenagers. We have never been collectors of furniture or objects, we both make things so we don't tend to acquire much. It remains a place of work, we never try to make it feel homey. In New York work is your joy, you love it. All your friends work in the same field. I think that's what gives New York its spark – it is so professional, which makes it very intense.' The space is indeed crammed with work, especially Ruben's whimsical, unexpected pieces – more often than not with Isabel's face smiling out serenely.

Isabel & Ruben Toledo

On the opening pages: a portrait of Ruben and Isabel Toledo, with Ruben's drawings in the background; and a detail of the ornate wrought-iron staircase that descends into the main studio space. *Opposite:* the wonderfully proportioned, high-ceilinged space, with its sash windows, tiled floor and 1950s table and chairs, can be used for working or entertaining. *Above:* a detail of the view from the apartment, showing the burnished roof of a neighbouring cupola. Isabel Toledo designed the canvas chair covers. The Italian teacups are part of a collection of idiosyncratic, brightly coloured pieces.

Right: a view of the main workroom space. In the foreground is Ruben's worktable. On the easel to the right is *Portrait of Isabel*, 1989; to the left is *Isabel*, 1991. Ruben also designed the black iron mannequins, to show selected pieces of the clothing that his wife designs. The cutouts of women's heads were made for the exhibition 'Tokyo Girls' in 1990. The bookcases were made to measure to hold the couple's vast collection of fashion and art books. *Above:* a view of the Empire State building, as seen from the main studio, through the skylight which is original to the space.

In Calvin Tsao and Zack McKown's apartment, a white plaster stairway curls upwards like the whorl of a shell, a stainless steel bath is gently shaped to fit the reclined body, while a large number of perfectly disguised cupboards serve to stow away the mess and clutter of daily life. Their Upper West Side duplex thus combines sensuality and minimalism in a particularly pleasing manner; it is not difficult to deduce that they are architects. However, although committed to the clean lines and precise beauty of pure architectural form, they are also drawn to rare fabrics, soft contours and classic twentieth-century furniture as well as the weird and wonderful things that they have collected during their travels. The space they share is a happy combination of these dichotomies. It should be added that they originally came from very different aesthetic backgrounds: Tsao was born in Hong Kong and lived there until the age of twelve, while Zack had a less exotic American upbringing. The two met when pitched together on a joint project at architecture school. They both really wanted to do their own thing and initially were reluctant to join up, but

26

after a stormy semester eventually turned in a successful project. 'I guess we both thought it was a let-down to have to compromise our vision with someone else – but here we still are, still collaborating …' laughs Tsao. Their 1929 home is in one of those majestic old apartment blocks on Central Park West. Overlooking the park and the American Museum of Natural History, their home enjoys south light all day long, which gives a marked chiaroscuro effect to the interior. Like the famous Dakota and San Remo buildings, both nearby, their block is derived from a European model but grafted onto the reality of 1920s and 30s America. Inside Tsao and McKown's space, however, that period's contained, urban 'cocktail lounge–jazz age' feel has been replaced by a different American blueprint. 'Both of us are from small towns so we loved the idea of living in an apartment with the soul of a house. It was interesting to take the memory of the organization of a house with a central stair and transform it; we also grafted on our experience of loft living, which led us to make the downstairs into one big flowing space.' This, unsurprisingly, led to accusations that the pair had turned some perfectly good New York real estate into a pastiche of a loft, but they continued their restructuring unperturbed. 'As architects, we always think of our residential work as portraiture; we ask ourselves, "If these people were houses, what would they look like?" Since this project was actually for us, it became quite an exercise in psychology!' Their approach to architecture is seemingly reductive, but beneath the surface all is not so clear-cut: opening a cupboard, for instance, becomes an experience, revealing the hidden world within. 'At the end of the day, this house is all about revealing and concealing,' Tsao remarks. 'It's kind of about closets.'

Calvin Tsao & Zack McKown

On the opening pages: a portrait of Calvin Tsao and Zack
McKown; and a detail of their staircase, which is sinuously
crafted to look like the interior whorl of a seashell. *Above:*
another view of the staircase, seen here from the kitchen,
showing the built-in dining table in the background. On the
table is a Chinese bowl of a type traditionally used for growing
narcissus, especially at Chinese New Year. The chairs are 1920s,
by Lafon. The candelabra are 1940s, and the unusual lamp is
an antique hospital appliance. *Opposite:* the cupboards, which
are usually kept firmly closed, are filled with Tsao and
McKown's beloved finds from around the world.

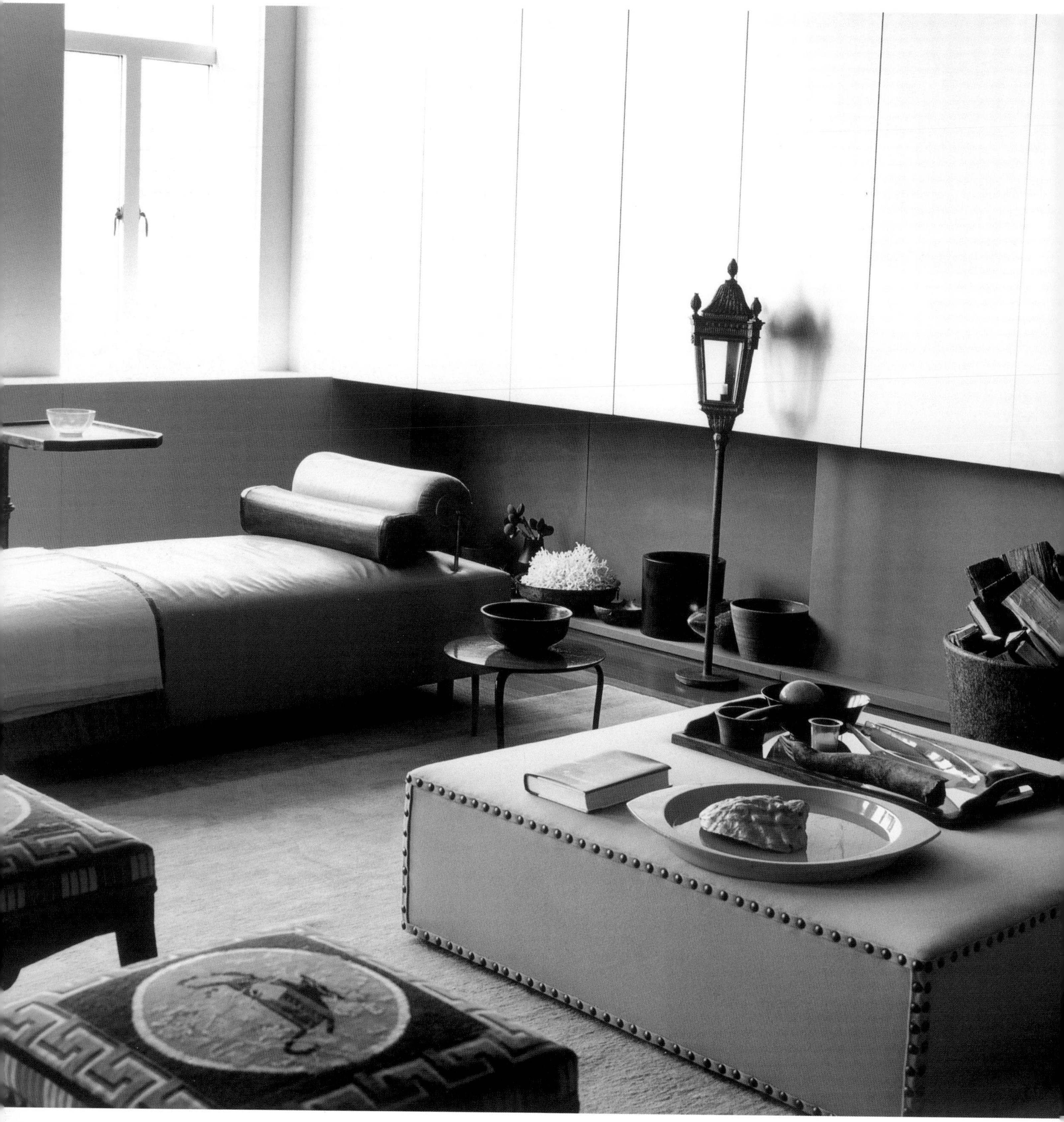

Opposite: a view of the living room showing the pewter-coloured wall, in palladium leaf, and the long low hearth. The daybed is a prototype from the 1940s; the yellow silk was bought in Bhutan. The stools are French Empire and are covered in *petit point* embroidery. The pouffe-cum-coffee table was made to Tsao and McKown's own design, while the lamp came originally from a Venetian gondola. *On this page:* the dressing room, left, was designed luxuriously to accommodate Calvin's entire wardrobe. It adjoins the bedroom, below. The silk counterpane is French eighteenth-century and the cushion is Turkish, acquired during a trip to Istanbul. The photograph over the bed, entitled *Cloud*, is by Richard Misrach.

On these pages: the rooms shown here have all been fitted in brushed steel, a material that Tsao and McKown have enjoyed exploring. The bathroom, above, features an unusual sink and an even more original bath, both designed by Tsao and McKown; the bath is ergonomically shaped to fit the reclining body. The wc, left, features heavy felt hangings on either side of a slit window and specially made brushed steel fittings. The kitchen, opposite, is on the ground floor, just off the dining room. The cooker hob has been fitted into a niche to make it more discreet. The brightly coloured bowls are by Tsao and McKown's friend Christian Perrochon.

The Provence-born artist Bernar Venet owns another house: a converted mill in the south of France, which snoozes under the Mediterranean sun and the generous shade of a plane tree while the mill stream froths under a picturesque bridge nearby. A handful of houses are huddled together in the hamlet, which has its own chateau as well as the Venets' perfectly proportioned home. The tableau sounds almost too good to be true, and anything that compels the Venets to leave this conventional version of paradise must be very powerful. Diane Venet, the artist's wife, laughs at the suggestion. 'Yes,' she acknowledges, 'like New York grit …'. Bernar has lived mainly in New York since 1966, when he lodged first on fellow French artist Arman's floor and then, rather fittingly, at the Chelsea Hotel, the notorious rock & roll haunt not far from the converted 1930s chocolate factory that the couple now call home. They moved there in 1997 when the place was an abandoned industrial property, and Chelsea was only just beginning to experience its current art-gallery-fuelled renaissance. The factory had what Diane considered essential attributes: a ground-floor

27

space to show some of Bernar's most monumental pieces, which weigh up to 10 tons; an office space; a studio, and a top-floor apartment with – luxury among luxuries – potential for a rooftop garden. They signed for the desolate-looking shell within twenty-four hours of their first visit. Then, the challenge was to make the domestic section into a real home, a task that was not made easier by the artist's refusal of such conventional comfort-inducers as carpeting and upholstered furniture. Luckily, Venet's talents are wide-ranging. While he first became established as a conceptual artist in the early 1960s, today his art is impossible to pigeonhole or label: as well as a sculptor he considers himself a musician, movie-maker, draughtsman, choreographer and, to all intents and purposes, an interior designer – at least as far as his own living spaces are concerned. 'Bernar did all the conception and drawing of the space, and designed almost all the furniture. He introduced the curved walls and the atrium, together with the cleverly placed bathroom that overlooks the greenery of the courtyard. In the end he succeeded in giving it an astonishingly intimate feel. It's big, but you never feel lost.' It may be a minimalist space, but it is also a charged environment. The house is stuffed with masses of rusty bars and forcefully bent steel. Highly provocative in its scale and rawness, this is Venet's own work. Every wall is covered with works by icons of modern art such as Frank Stella, Mark Rothko, Donald Judd, Sol LeWitt and Ellsworth Kelly; each room, simply decorated in white, provides a foil for potent pieces by artist friends. As with most creative talents, Venet's art is unsegregated from his life: the presence of his restless, roaming intelligence can be felt on every surface and in every room.

Diane & Bernar Venet

On the opening pages: a portrait of Diane Venet in her verdant interior courtyard; and a view of the façade of the ex-chocolate factory in Chelsea, its loading-bay doors open to reveal Bernar Venet's sculptures. *On the previous double page:* the ground-floor loading dock seen from the inside, showing three of Venet's *Indeterminate Line* sculptures in rusted steel. *Above:* the sofas and coffee table were designed by Venet. On the wall are two drawings from 1998. The sculpture on the coffee table is *Four Arcs of 235.5°*, also from 1998. *Left:* the bedroom, with a mural by Lawrence Weiner. *Opposite:* the dining area, with a table designed by Bernar Venet. The black painting is also by Venet; the prints in the kitchen beyond are by Donald Judd.

ACKNOWLEDGEMENTS

I put this book together under the benevolent guidance and
master eye of aesthete extraordinaire Hamish Bowles, whose acute
comments, based on his experience of Manhattan living – which is
much greater than mine – helped me to achieve the cross-section
of interiors that make up this book.

I must first and foremost thank the photographers: Alberto Heras,
understanding comrade, companion and accomplice; and Graham
Kuhn, hospitable and generous friend in need during the whole
of my New York experience. Olivier Gelbsmann styled the Muriel
Brandolini shoot, and was most helpful.

Lesley Simitch, introduced to me by my dear friend Pamela Hanson,
went way beyond the call of duty in sharing with me her vast
experience of locations in the city with great good humour. Kathy
Korvin and Anh Duong gave me much good and solid advice, which
formed the backbone of the project. My friend Patrick Deedes Vinke
and his associate Oliver Hicks from Lighthouse were also very
helpful indeed, and provided wonderful moral support.

Many people advised me as to the interiors to be included: Erica
Lennard, with her characteristic generosity; Kim Hastreiter, Editor-
in-Chief of the cutting-edge *Paper* magazine, whose finger is most
definitely on the pulse of the city and who made only great
suggestions; André Walker, the fashion designer who introduced me
to Kim in the first place; Holly Solomon, who was unfailingly helpful
and kind, as was the photographer David Seidner. My heartfelt
thanks go to Suzanne Slesin, the doyenne of the world of interiors,
who kindly encouraged me and even trusted me to photograph
her house; my friend Tara Abate who gave excellent advice, and
also to Linda O'Keefe, another seasoned professional, for her
encouragement. Gwenn Williams at Julian Schnabel's studio
was wonderfully efficient.

Linda Heras and Robert Angel both contributed to the book with
their practical advice and help.

Last but not least my colleagues and assistants: Miriam Almanzar,
who was most inspirational on the subject of the city she loves
beyond all others; Anna Vidal, who did a lot of the groundwork by
phone and fax and did most of the transcribing, with her usual
charm; and Anna Kostritzky who did on-site work in New York.
The original prints were by Antonio Garcia for Duplifoto, Madrid.

Finally thank you to my wonderful agent Maggie Philips, and to my
copy-editor Christine Davis.

BIBLIOGRAPHY

Allen, Irving Lewis. *The City in Slang*. (Oxford University Press, 1993.)

Anderson, Jervis. *This Was Harlem: A Cultural Portrait*. (Farrar, Straus & Giroux, 1982.)

Barth, Gunther. *City People: The Rise of Modern City Culture in Nineteenth-Century America*. (Oxford University Press, 1980.)

Campbell, Nina, and Caroline Seebohm. *Elise de Wolfe: A Decorative Life*. (Potter, 1992.)

Cantwell, Mary. *Manhattan, When I was Young*. (Penguin Books, 1996.)

Chesterton, G.K. *What I Saw in America*. (Dodd, Mead & Company, 1922.)

Cole, William. *Quotable New York: A Literary Companion*. (Penguin Books, 1993.)

Fodor's New York City. (Fodor's Travel Publications, 1993.)

Garcia Lorca, Federico. *Poet in New York*. (The Noonday Press, 1988.)

Janowitz, Tama. *Slaves of New York*. (Crown Publishers, 1986.)

Lankevitch, George L. *American Metropolis: A History of New York City*. (New York University Press, 1998.)

Lewis, David Levering. *When Harlem was in Vogue*. (Knopf, 1981.)

McInerney, Jay. *Bright Lights, Big City*. (Vintage, 1984.)

Miller, Terry. *Greenwich Village and How It Got That Way*. (Crown Publishers, 1990.)

Mitchell, Joseph. *Up in the Old Hotel*. (Vintage, 1993.)

Morris, Lloyd. *Incredible New York: High Life and Low Life of The Last Hundred Years*. (Syracuse University Press, 1996; orig. pub.1951.)

Norris, Kathleen. *Leaving New York: Writers Look Back*. (Hungry Mind Press, 1995.)

Scott Fitzgerald, F. *Afternoon of an Author*. (The Scribner Library, 1957.)

Stansell, Christine. *City of Women: Sex and Class in New York, 1789–1860*. (Knopf, 1986.)

Still, Bayrd. *Mirror for Gotham: New York as Seen by Contemporaries from Dutch Days to the Present*. (New York University Press, 1956.)

Taylor, William R., ed. *In Pursuit of Gotham: Culture and Commerce in New York*. (Oxford University Press, 1992.)

Wharton, Edith. *A Backward Glance*. (Everyman 1993, orig. pub. 1934.)

Whitman, Walt (ed. John Kouwenhoven). *Leaves of Grass and Selected Prose*. (Modern Library, 1950.)